# Praise for *Overload:*

"This is a brilliant treatment which should sensitize others and educate the ADDer about how to prepare for and avoid overwhelming situations. . . . there are tons of good ideas, advice for parents, educators, ADDers (addicts or not), as well as resources and contacts for continued learning."

**John Ratey, M.D., author of *Driven to Distraction* and *Shadow Syndromes***

"This is an extraordinary and fascinating book. The bridging of both the clinical and biogenetic aspects is a landmark accomplishment for works on this very complex disorder. This is one of the most important works on this subject in the last ten years."

**David Smith, M.D., President, American Society of Addiction Medicine**

# Overload

## Attention Deficit Disorder and the Addictive Brain

By David K. Miller
and Kenneth Blum, Ph.D.

**Andrews and McMeel**

A Universal Press Syndicate Company
Kansas City

Library of Congress Cataloging-in-Publication Data
Miller, David K.
Overload : attention deficit disorder and the addictive brain /
by David K. Miller and Kenneth Blum.
p.    cm.
Includes bibliographical references.
ISBN 0-8362-0460-3 (pb)
1. Attention-deficit disorder in adults.  2. Substance abuse—Etiology.
3. Alcoholism—Etiology.  4. Stimulus compounding.
5. Alcoholism—Relapse—Prevention.
6. Substance abuse—Relapse—Prevention.
I. Blum, Kenneth. II. Title.
RC394.A85M55  1996
616.85'89—dc20   95-46311
CIP

First Printing, February 1996
Third Printing, September 1997

---

**Attention: Schools and Businesses**

Andrews and McMeel books are available at quantity discounts
with bulk purchase for educational, business, or sales
promotional use. For information, please write to:
Special Sales Department, Andrews and McMeel,
4520 Main Street, Kansas City, Missouri 64111.

## To Merlene Miller and James E. Payne

for their contribution to the writing of this book.
They helped us put together our thoughts and words
in a way we alone never could have. Without their
dedication, writing skills, and hard work our
ideas might still be mere conversations rather
than enduring words on a page.

# Contents

❖
_____

# Acknowledgments

We want to thank the many people who helped make this book possible. We wish to acknowledge the professional contributions of Dale Walters, Rick Thomas, Carol Cummings, Kathy Sloan, Jack Johnson, Eric Braverman, Hans Huessy, Jim Payne, David E. Comings, John C. Call, and Marilyn Shank. A special thank-you to Jean Lowe who is our editor and, more than that, our friend. Other friends and family whose support and help we deeply appreciate are Peter Sheridan, Anne Welch, Anne Barcus, Lloyd and Jean Hurshman, Christene Kelly, Dave and Julie Womeldorf, Lisa Havens, Janet Voss, Stephen Emerick, Sue Kennard, Merle and Cleona Guthrie, Rick Mast, Jon Stover, Becky Paffen, and Dan Miller.

The personal stories in this book are from real people. Some names have been changed, some stories have been altered somewhat, and some are composites of more than one person. But they have all come from the hearts of those who have experienced them. We want to thank those who were willing to share with us and our readers: Carol, Anne, Tim, John, Mike, Brad, Sheila, Becky, Allison, Kathy, Hannah, Tricia, Paul, Doug, Mike, Jon, David, Martha, Matt, Julie, Jean, and Andy.

We especially want to give loving thanks to our wives, Merlene Miller and Arlene Blum, and our sons: Jeffrey Blum and Seth Blum; Greg Sloan (and his family); Clark Sloan (and his family); Brad Miller; and Doug Sloan.

We would like to pay special tribute to the following people. David: my mother, Lois Watts, whose unconditional love has instilled in me hope, courage, and faith in myself to keep on keeping on. Kenneth: My parents, Lena and Harry, and my loving sister, Barbara, who all provided the framework from which I could give of myself unconditionally.

# Introduction

I have been working in the addiction field as a clinician for about seventeen years. A lot has changed in that time, not only with me but also in this field of study. When I first started working as a counselor, the term "disease concept" was just beginning to be used in reference to alcoholism, with the emphasis on *concept*. There was still a question about whether this was a physiological condition or just a character defect. But research was beginning to give us reason to believe there were some people who were physically predisposed to becoming addicted to alcohol.

Because of the experience of thousands of people, we did know that recovery from alcoholism required abstinence from alcohol, indicating that for some people there is a physiological reaction to alcohol that is different from the reaction of those who can drink in moderation. In treatment, what was primarily emphasized was what happened when people were still drinking, the goal being abstinence. And it was assumed that once people accepted that they had a disease and that they needed to stop drinking, then the physical symptoms of their addiction went away. The supposition was that if they relapsed, it was for psychological reasons.

It was recognized, of course, that there were some early physical withdrawal symptoms—for three days to a week—and some craving when people first stopped drinking or using other drugs. If people could get through that early withdrawal and the craving, then they could live in comfortable sobriety and prevent relapse if they practiced a recovery program that addressed psychological and spiritual needs.

But I was finding in the people I was counseling, as well as in my own personal experience, that craving was not the only abstinence-based symptom to addiction. I was fortunate in my career to work with Terry Gorski who had done research into what causes people to relapse. From that research and other research that was emerging at the time, it became apparent that there are symptoms of addiction that occur *after* the early withdrawal symptoms go away.

Terry referred to these symptoms as post-acute withdrawal symptoms because it was believed at that time that these symptoms were due to the damage done to the nervous system by alcohol or other drugs and that they diminished over time and usually disappeared six months to two years into sobriety.

My experience as a counselor verified that there was a relationship between these symptoms and relapse, that people who experienced more severe post-acute withdrawal symptoms were more inclined to relapse. My patients who relapsed described a very uncomfortable sobriety. Getting sober and getting past the early withdrawal and the craving didn't do it for them. As time went on, they became *more* uncomfortable.

My wife, Merlene, Terry, and I wrote a book, *Learning to Live Again, A Guide to Recovery from Alcoholism* (recently updated and titled *Learning to Live Again, A Guide to Recovery from Chemical Dependency),* in which we described post-acute withdrawal, ways to reduce the severity of the symptoms and increase the enjoyment of life in recovery. Merlene and Terry later wrote a book, *Staying Sober,* about preventing relapse.

In these books, post-acute withdrawal symptoms are listed as problems with concentration and memory, emotional overreaction, thought process problems, sleep disturbances, and stress sensitivity. In *Staying Sober,* particularly, these symptoms are linked with relapse. The more severe these symptoms, the more likely people are to relapse because they are in pain and are looking for relief. Even if they are not consciously aware of it, they know what will make them feel better. They are aware that it is the drug or the chemical that they have given up that will relieve their pain.

As I observed these symptoms in my clients, I became convinced that the symptoms didn't go away in six to twenty-four months as we had been saying. My clients began to say to me, "I've been sober for six years and I'm still having trouble with memory, concentration, and especially with my overreaction to stress—my moods swings and my low frustration tolerance."

And many of my clients began to say, "Yes, I have these symptoms, but my alcoholism didn't cause them. That's why I started drinking, because I was like this before I started drinking. There is something that was different about me from the time I was a child. I have always known I was different—and when I began to drink (or when I began to use drugs), I said, 'Hey, this is what I've been looking for.' I felt so much better when I was drinking and using and all those symptoms went away. But my use of alcohol and drugs didn't cause the symptoms."

So I began to think these were not *withdrawal* symptoms. I referred to them less and less as post-acute *withdrawal* and more often as sobriety-based symptoms or abstinence-based symptoms. I no longer believed that they were always caused by drug use, though I was convinced they were *intensified* by the use of the drugs and that they were more severe when people stopped using than they had been prior to use.

I have to acknowledge that many of my clients were people who had relapsed. Because of working with Terry, and because of his work on relapse, there was a tendency for me to have a higher percentage of relapse clients than another addiction counselor might have. So to say that everybody who is recovering experiences these symptoms is not true. But the majority of my clients identified with these symptoms and most had relapsed, not because they weren't motivated but because they were in so much pain. Their relapse was not an indication that they didn't value sobriety; it was an indication that they had held on for as long as they could and needed some relief.

Certainly, many of my clients with these symptoms *hadn't* relapsed. Some were hanging on, some were finding healthy ways to feel good, and some were finding harmful ways to feel good. Some overate, some gambled, some worked, and some went to movies—excessively. Most people who stop drinking alcohol increase their consumption of nicotine, sugar, and caffeine. It's a substitute way to feel good.

Somewhere along this path of looking at these symptoms, I came across some research that indicated the majority of people recovering from alcoholism experience stimulus augmentation.[1] This has been described as an amplification of sensory input, an overreaction to the environment—to noise, light, touch. It is related to an inability to filter incoming stimuli so that it is difficult to focus attention in any one place. As soon as I read about it I realized that "stimulus augmentation" gave me a name for something I had experienced all my life—the sensation that the world's volume level is turned up. I also learned that for people who have this condition, drinking or taking drugs turns down the volume.[2] This certainly had been the case for me.

I began to talk to clients about stimulus augmentation. And when I did, they usually looked at me as though I had described a hidden secret. They had thought there was something uniquely wrong with them. They were relieved to have someone not only describe what they could not but assure them that the condition is common among recovering people. But frequently they said they had had it all their lives. It was not something that developed because they got addicted to drugs and then sobered up. It wasn't caused by their drug use. Sometimes people who were not addicted told me they had stimulus augmentation. But often when I asked if either of their parents were alcoholics, they said yes.

I talked more and more about the importance of addressing stimulus augmentation in recovery. As I did, I began to hear other professionals say, "I work with children with attention deficit hyperactivity disorder and they have this." I heard this so often that I began to wonder if there was a connection between attention deficit hyperactivity disorder, stimulus augmentation, and addiction. Since stimulus augmentation seemed to be a symptom that was very common in both groups of people, I began to look for the connection. This was what led me to my own diagnosis of attention deficit hyperactivity disorder.

As I read more about it, I learned that:

1. Significantly more children with attention deficit hyperactivity disorder (ADHD) develop problems with alcoholism or drug addiction than do children without ADHD.[3]

2. Alcoholics frequently have a history of childhood hyperactivity.[4]

3. People who become alcoholics show a much higher frequency of symptoms of ADHD as children than those who do not become alcoholics.[5]

4. Children of alcoholics have been shown to perform poorly on tests measuring attention, memory, perceptual-motor coordination, motor speed, spatial sequencing, and language capacity.[6]

5. Studies show that alcoholics have impaired verbal learning and memory[7] and exhibit various other deficits[8] similar to what has been observed in children of alcoholics. This indicates that these impairments may have preceded drinking onset.[9]

6. Many people with ADHD are children of alcoholics[10] and ADHD is common in the relatives of ADHD children.[11]

7. Sons of alcoholics have been found to magnify perceptual input.[12]

8. In alcoholics, stimulus augmentation has been demonstrated to be related to a strong motivation or craving to obtain alcoholic beverages.[13]

9. Up to one-third of alcoholics meet the criteria for a diagnosis of attention deficit hyperactivity disorder.[14]

10. Children of alcoholics are at high risk of becoming addicted.[15]

11. Sensory information is often amplified in addicts before they start taking drugs.[16]

12. Stimulus augmentation is common in children of alcoholics.[17]

With all this related evidence it seemed reasonable to believe that, in many cases, ADHD and addiction were connected genetically. My search eventually took me to Dr. Kenneth Blum, the coauthor of this book, who was doing research on brain chemistry and addiction. I found that Ken had come to the same conclusion from scientific research that I had come to from clinical experience: There is a large group of people who have both conditions and it is likely that in many cases the conditions are genetically connected.

One reason this connection was not observed sooner is that it was not known that adults had attention deficit hyperactivity disorder. We didn't look for it in adults because we thought children outgrew it. It has only become known in the last few years that some do not outgrow attention deficit hyperactivity disorder in adolescence. I personally believe that *most* don't outgrow it.

Perhaps, I thought, the reason it was believed for so long that children outgrew ADHD was that self-medicating with alcohol or other drugs in adolescence worked so well to relieve the symptoms that their ADHD seemed to have disappeared. It stands to reason, then, that the symptoms would come back in sobriety. I began recognizing ADHD in a number of my clients. When I encouraged them to get diagnosed and when we treated both ADHD and their addiction, many found relief from the "abstinence-based symptoms" that had made sobriety such a struggle.

Yes, much of the research done on attention deficit hyperactivity disorder, stimulus augmentation, and addiction—when put together—supports the concept that they are connected. That does not mean that all people with attention deficit hyperactivity disorder become addicted, or that all people who are addicted have attention deficit hyperactivity disorder, or that everyone who has post-acute withdrawal symptoms or stimulus augmentation has attention deficit hyperactivity disorder. We don't want to get carried away and make assumptions that cannot be supported with the facts. Sobriety can be uncomfortable for many people who don't have ADHD. They might have some of these same symptoms, but for them the symptoms *are* caused by drug use.

But a large number of recovering people, especially those that are relapse-prone, have undiagnosed attention deficit hyperactivity disorder and need treatment for their attention deficit hyperactivity disorder in order to fully recover from their addiction. And children of alcoholics and children with attention deficit are at high risk of becoming addicted. We must recognize this truth and address it in order to reduce significantly the serious problem of drug use and addiction.

David Miller

# Introduction
## The Scientific Viewpoint

I have been involved in scientific pharmaceutical exploration for over twenty-five years. I was born in Brooklyn and grew up in an orthodox Jewish home with loving parents and one sister. After graduating from college, I married my wife, Arlene, and have two children, Seth and Jeff. My life was filled with love and happiness without much distress at all. My first interaction with the world of drugs came when I entered Columbia University College of Pharmacy where I developed a strong interest in research. Following my graduation I entered New Jersey College of Medicine, graduating with a degree in medical science.

Following a small stint at U.S. Vitamin Pharmaceutical Corporation where I served as chief neuropharmacologist, I entered New York University to receive a Ph.D. in neuropharmacology. I studied under the direction of Joseph Siefter who was the former director of all research for Wyeth Laboratories, the company that developed the first use of tranquilizers in America. I did my Ph.D. thesis on a substance that has become quite popular, Carnitine (vitamin BT). I found that this substance mimics the action of acetycholine, a chemical in the brain. As my interest turned toward psychopharmacology, instead of entering medical school in New York City for my M.D. degree (with encouragement from a former professor of mine, Irving Geller, and from my mentor Joseph Siefter), I found myself in San Antonio at the Southwest Foundation working as a senior research scientist in the division of behavioral sciences.

At that time, in 1968, I had no interest at all in alcohol pharmacology or alcoholism. But that was the year a new institute arrived on the American scene, the National Institute of Alcoholism and Alcohol Abuse. With some reluctance, Dr. Geller and I requested a grant from the institute to show effects of stress on alcohol intake in animals and on related brain chemicals. The individual who reviewed the grant and visited our laboratory was Ernest Noble, a man who not only became a colleague but has been a friend for over twenty-five years. He happened to be working on brain chemical relationships similar to what we were proposing.

In order to explain how, through my own research, I came to the same conclusion as my coauthor, David Miller, I would like you to come with me into my laboratory in an attempt to understand my research position. To begin with, we found that animals exposed to stress drank large amounts of alcohol only on the weekend when there was no stress. It was as if we were looking at a human binge drinker, and we had no explanation for this phenomenon. We felt that one explanation for this surprising result was that during the weekend when the lights were turned off, darkness had something to do with the drinking. Following a quick trip to Atlantic City where we listened to Nobel Prize–winner Julius Axelrod discuss circadian rhythm, Geller placed rats in a dark closet and found copious drinking in rats that hated alcohol.

I later conducted a number of experiments at the University of Texas Health Science Center relating to what factors increased or reduced alcohol craving in rats. This research turned me on to the idea that craving for alcohol is related to chemicals in the brain.

In 1970, while I was still at the Southwest Foundation, Virginia Davis and Michael Walsh published the first paper suggesting that when an animal drinks alcohol, it produces a substance called tetrahydropapaveroline (THP). The interesting thing about this is that this substance is also found in the poppy plant, from which morphine is synthesized. Davis and Walsh suggested that there may be something biochemically similar in the executive alcoholic and the junkie shooting heroin in the street. Following this exciting study, Jerry Cohen and Michael Collings at Columbia found another type of isoquinoline salsolinol (TIQ) in animals drinking alcohol, further indicating that there is a reaction in the brain when alcohol is consumed that is similar to the reaction to opiates, such as morphine and heroin.

At that time, my laboratory began to explore this alcohol/opiate connection. We were the first laboratory to show that a narcotic antagonist, naloxone, or, later, naltrexone, (now called ReVia and produced by Du Pont), blocked alcohol-induced sleep in mice. We went on to show that by using this narcotic antagonist in mice we could block alcohol-induced dependence. We also found that if you give an alcohol-drinking rat a narcotic antagonist you could significantly reduce the intake of alcohol.

We found the first evidence that the brain chemical dopamine can block withdrawal from alcohol in rodents. This effect was found by administering morphine to alcohol-abstinent mice, which resulted in prolonged blocking of abstinence symptoms similar to the dopamine response. For over ten years our laboratory was devoted to understanding how TIQ could act as an alcohol-like substance as well as an opiatelike substance. Indeed, we found that TIQ could enhance alcohol-induced sleep in mice, reduce alcohol withdrawal reactions in mice, and potentiate morphine-induced analgesic response.

We forwarded a sample of TIQ to the laboratory of Avram Goldstein at Stanford, following the discovery and isolation of an opiate receptor. To his great surprise, the TIQ specifically bound to the opiate receptor. This original work was confirmed here in the United States and in Italy.

In conjunction with my colleague Maurice Hirst from the University of London–Ontario in Canada and a graduate student, Murry Hamilton, who came to Texas to work with me, we found the first metabolite of TIQ, providing a way to measure TIQ in the brain. Based on all this research we suggested and provided evidence for linking TIQ to both alcohol and opiates.

By 1978 I had a strong interest in pharmacogenetics. I entered the University of Colorado Institute of Behavioral Genetics to train with Gerald McLearn, the father of modern animal genetics of alcoholism, and his colleagues. Following an eight-week intensive fellowship, we developed the concept known as the "psychogenetic theory of drug craving."

Back at the University of Texas Health Science Center we performed a number of experiments in genetically bred mice having different preferences for alcohol (some loved alcohol and some hated alcohol). Our thought was that animals born with low levels of the substance endorphin should have a higher preference for alcohol than animals born with high levels of endorphins. Our findings were published and later verified by other investigators.

Another important finding related to the fact that when animals drink alcohol chronically over a long period of time they shut off the synthesis of endorphins in the brain bringing about a deficiency. An experiment was done at the University of Ohio suggesting that when animals are stressed (allowed to swim in ice-cold water) they drink higher amounts of alcohol, and this is correlated with a reduced amount of endorphins in the brain. These three experiments together suggested that alcohol craving was linked to endorphin function in the brain.

In 1981 we began to explore ways we could alter alcohol intake by manipulating the endorphin system. At that time we found that if we injected D-Phenylalanine, an amino acid that inhibits the breakdown of endorphins in the brain, we could virtually wipe out craving for alcohol in animals that loved it. In 1984 I was approached by a number of people in Houston to develop a small pharmaceutical company based on this discovery.

During this period a number of researchers found that drug craving was linked to abnormalities found in the neurotransmitter system of the brain. The substances involved were serotonin, the endorphins, an inhibitory substance called GABA, and dopamine. My goal at that time was to develop a nutritional supplement that would restore the balance in the brain of humans who ingested alcohol or who had a predisposition to craving behavior based on a genetic deficiency, which was unknown to us at the time. We felt that the key to overcoming craving could be found in the brain and probably had to do with an endorphin deficiency.

**Introduction: The Scientific Viewpoint**

A number of nutritional supplements were developed to assist patients in their attempt to achieve high-quality recovery. I spent the next five years carrying out clinical trials with a number of colleagues throughout the United States to determine the efficacy of nutritional supplements not only for alcoholism but also for cocaine craving and carbohydrate bingeing. I believe this was the first attempt to utilize amino acid therapy in conjunction with a substance that had enkephalinase inhibitory properties (blocking the enzyme that destroys endorphins).

We then developed the concept of the *reward cascade* which brought together the understanding of how a number of chemicals could interact in the brain and ultimately lead to dopamine release and reward of good feelings or the "feel good response" (FGR). In 1988 we decided to embark on an experiment that ultimately led to discovery of the first specific molecular link to alcoholism. This work was done with my colleagues at the University of Texas, especially Peter Sheridan and my colleague Ernest Noble at the University of California–Los Angeles. We found a gene connected to alcoholism—the D2 receptor gene. The importance of this finding was that it generated a tremendous amount of interest in the media and probably had a great effect on reducing the stigma associated with alcoholism.

Many experiments since this initial finding in 1990 have found the D2 receptor gene to be associated with a variety of impulsive, compulsive, and addictive behaviors, including polysubstance dependence, crack cocaine, smoking, carbohydrate bingeing, pathological gambling, and, most important, behavioral conditions such as Tourette syndrome, post-traumatic stress disorder, and attention deficit hyperactivity disorder. Realizing that there was a common underlying genetic route to all these behaviors, we decided to give a name to this complex condition. The name I chose—*reward deficiency syndrome* (RDS)—related to the deficiency in the reward part of the brain where dopamine works.

Five years after discovering this genetic connection we are pleased to announce the development of a DNA-based test to allow for early identification or predisposition to *reward deficiency syndrome* and associated addictive, impulsive, and compulsive behaviors. This is not to say there is only one gene associated with RDS.[1] We feel sure that we are just beginning to uncover what we need to know about addiction and behavioral disorders. In fact, there are at least three dopaminergic genes associated with RDS (dopamine D2 receptor, dopamine transporter, and dopamine Beta-hydroxylase genes).

While this work was going on, I got a call from my coauthor, David Miller, who had read my book, *Alcohol and the Addictive Brain*. He suggested to me that individuals with attention deficit hyperactivity disorder have high rates of subsequent alcohol- and drug-seeking behavior followed by postabstinence symptoms indicating that addiction does not disappear when drug use stops.

I told David at that time that his thinking was, in my mind, absolutely correct and that I also had come to the same conclusion, not clinically, but through the empirical research I have just described. I met with David and his wife, Merlene, at a Texas Commission on Alcoholism meeting where she was speaking. At once we were compelled to bring together David's view as a clinician specializing in addiction (who also has ADHD) with my view as a scientist. Our conviction was that ADHD was indeed an important precursor to a life of despair and potential addiction to mood-altering drugs. The writing of this book is the result of our continued communication on this issue.

Kenneth Blum, Ph.D.

# 1

## The Fly on the Wall Down the Hall Is Driving Me Crazy: David's Story

It was with a tremendous rush of relief and excitement and with a whirlwind of mixed emotions that I finally confronted the mysterious force that had plagued my life. It now had a name: attention deficit hyperactivity disorder. It explained so much: the childhood problems that had followed me into adulthood, my alcoholism and the difficulty of my recovery, the inability to organize and manage my life.

My life had been a series of beginnings without endings, projects started and never finished. Looking back I realized I had left unfinished many more tasks than I had ever finished. Somewhere out there in the "unfinished task boneyard" lay hundreds of pieces of model airplanes and Erector sets, wood intended for a fort, incomplete assignments, articles half-read, letters half-written, conversations half-listened to, and wonderful book titles and ideas conjured up but never used.

It was fatiguing to think of all the opportunities I had passed up over the years because I could not focus on the steps of learning—thousands of ideas never followed through, wonderful ideas that were never given any dimension because they could not be taken far enough. From singing lessons to violin instruction. From organized sports to new, exciting, and challenging ventures. Oh, don't get me wrong. I got by, but that's part of the tragedy. I just got by. And in the process, so many opportunities and bits of good living were missed and so much energy was spent in coping that could have been used for productive, constructive, joyful living.

There were financial problems and some legal problems because I had not taken care of matters on time. I had let people down because I could not meet their expectations. I had regrets because of impulsive decisions I had made. In many ways my life was a series of disappointments, poor choices, and missed opportunities.

But I was now at the moment where my poison was finally named. After all the years of pinning my problems to myriad other reasons, I was diagnosed with attention deficit hyperactivity disorder (ADHD). Even though I had suspected such a diagnostic outcome, anticipating it was quite different from feeling its truth. Finally I had an answer for everyone who had ever asked me to diagnose myself, who had asked why I had done this and why I had said that and why I was like I was. Why didn't I listen? Why didn't I remember? Why couldn't I follow directions? Why did I drink excessively and why couldn't I stop when I started having problems because of it? Why couldn't I follow through on what I said I would do?

To my inquisitors I say, it wasn't me you saw. It was what was covering me up. You saw my defenses and compensations. You saw my reactions to an unknown attacker and the raper of my courage. You did not see the courageous survivor part of me attempting to make sense of my world, attempting to shine through the fog.

I never had an answer to what was wrong with me because I just did not know. Like everyone else, I had somehow believed that if I just tried harder I could make myself better. But if you are trying to pound in a nail with a marshmallow, it doesn't help to hit harder. Now I felt that perhaps I could apply the energy I had expended in attempting to fix myself to what I could do something about. The defenses I had used to protect myself from the whys now seemed to fall on the floor around me like a discarded skin no longer of use. Years of grief seemed to flow out in that instant like a dam of realization had burst as I relived the years of pain when nothing made sense and I had no answers and no explanations.

In one of my earliest memories I was about three years old, lying on my bed, eyes closed, rocking my head back and forth, groaning "uh, uh, uh, uh" with each movement—a kind of ritual chant to hold at bay the clamor of sounds making it impossible for me to go to sleep. Ordinary sounds. My twin brother, Dan, breathing in sleep in the bed next to mine. The radio playing in the living room. A dog barking. Everyday sounds unbearably amplified in my mind.

My chant didn't bother my brother. Nothing bothered him. But my mother heard me and came in to ask, as usual, "What's the matter, honey? Why aren't you sleeping?" and I couldn't tell her. I didn't know what the matter was. I just knew that rocking my head back and forth on the pillow and making the groaning noise helped to deaden the other noises that were beating at me, the overwhelming bombardment of sensations that didn't seem to bother other people but were painful for me.

The problem that dominated my life and shaped my personality was the need to avoid the piercing, rasping, blasting, disorganized chaos of incoming stimuli that I could not filter out, could not ignore. This made it hard for me to relate to other people; to think, study, and make it in school; to carry out tasks, plan ahead, remember. It embarrassed me and made me feel ashamed when I was with people; it made me insecure when I was alone.

My ability to shut out unwanted stimuli was challenged monthly by the meeting of my mother's sewing club in our home. I anticipated these gatherings with dread, knowing I would not be able to sleep. Not that they were rowdy or argumentative; the tiniest noise could keep me awake. I swear the buzzing of a fly on the wall down the hall could drive me crazy! So you can imagine what the noise from the overextended vocal cords of fifteen females did to my need for peace and quiet. Never once through what seemed to be a thousand years of sewing club did I fall asleep before it was over.

My sensitivity to all stimuli increased as I grew older. Indoors or out, the space around me seemed flooded with sounds that were too loud, lights and colors that were too bright, odors that were too intense, tastes that were too strong, touches that were too harsh. I could not shut them out. They were piercing and confusing.

Overload!

My brother and I were adopted. We didn't know our biological parents, but our adopted parents were our real parents and did their best for us. My mother wanted nothing more than to provide as much love as possible for her nonidentical twin boys. She had no insight into my problem, but she was as good to us as she knew how to be. She became a resource that I could depend on. She wanted to be a mother, and she was good at it. Dad wanted us, too, and he loved us. But he also wanted his alcohol, the alcohol that periodically turned our house into pandemonium. Today we would probably be termed "dysfunctional," but we were a loving family.

It irritated me that my brother, Dan, wasn't bothered at all by the things that bothered me. He seemed to have an uncanny ability to keep cool when I was bouncing off the wall. Most of the time Dan and I were good buddies; and hiking, fishing, hunting, and exploring with him provided the solace and healthy diversion I needed to make sense of my world. Dan was always a reassuring touchstone for me.

The differences between my brother and me were evident in how we dealt with school. He never had any problems; I think he even liked school, which seemed incomprehensible to me. He was so different from me I sometimes suspected that he was not my brother at all, that someone had made a mistake at the hospital. We even differed radically in how we walked. I marched and he just shuffled along. On the way to school I was always half a block ahead, begging him to hurry so we would not be late. (A neighbor witnessing this daily ritual appropriately nicknamed us "Pete" and "Repete.") I had a great fear of being late and of everyone looking at me as I entered class. Dan? He couldn't have cared less.

Why was I always in a hurry to get to school? It's hard to understand. Who wants to hurry to a place where there are only bad feelings, where the only good things to look forward to are recess and going home? Thinking back, I know now that hurrying was the only way I could deal with my fragmented perception of time. I thought my reason for hurrying was to give myself plenty of time to prepare for the day's drudgery, even though I knew it wouldn't help. But the real reason was that I simply didn't know how to stay in the present

## The Fly on the Wall

long enough to make friends with it. I had to barrel ahead like a bat out of hell because "fast forward" was the only gear I had.

My early school years were traumatic. The psychological abuse from teachers skewed my perception of my ability to learn as well as of the learning process itself. All the degrees in the world are not worth a second of the hell I endured during those days in Mrs. Retchit's classroom. Did her radar lock on to my acute sensitivity? Did I broadcast telltale signs of my deficiency before I even opened my mouth? I must have worn a big sign on my back visible only to Retchit: Please abuse me! Ask only me to go to the blackboard to do math because I want to be humiliated before Mrs. Retchit, God, and the world. It must have been there, and she must have read it every day because she always obliged. If you could have listened in on my thoughts as I trudged to the schoolhouse chamber of horrors on a typical school day, you would have heard something like this:

*Gotta hurry, gotta get there, come on, Dan, get your butt in gear. Stomach hurts, feels empty, can't barf, not sick enough to stay home today. Homework—as usual didn't do it. Gotta find a way to make this work. Did I forget my book? What can I say that will sound good? Gotta make it up, gotta make it do. Pants feel like hell, can't stand it, too baggy, not a part of me. What are those kids laughing at outside the school? Don't they know where they are? How can they have fun at a place like this? Inside at last. Here goes.*

As I breathe in the school odors—pencils, erasers, marble floors layered with wax and disinfectant, that funny red sawdust stuff, teacher's perfume, body odors, and the manure smell on the pants of the farm kids—I shudder, anticipating the worst.

Stomach bouncing, getting nearer to Retchit's domain, I find my carved-up huge desk looking exactly like all the other carved-up huge desks arranged neatly and expectantly, awaiting my terror, standing perfectly in line as symbols of the order of this industrial age. God, I would think, wherever you are, please see me through another day. Grant me the blessing of invisibility. He never did.

Retchit had X-ray vision. She could see my terror-stricken face through the chest of the classmate in front of me. The devil himself could not have inspired more dread than the words, "David, would you come up to the board today and demonstrate for the class how you solved the problem on page thirty-two of your workbook?" From that point on I was frozen in autopilot mode as if out of my body in a dream. Long before I could turn to page thirty-two to see what the problem was, my brain had shut down. The problem could have been "1 + 1," and I still would have blocked the answer. As I stared at the unsolved problem in my workbook, it looked huge, scattered all over the page.

When I took my detached, rubbery hand and scrawled the problem on the board, what I saw was complete gobbledegook. I could do nothing but squirm, twitch, sweat, and say stupid things as Retchit interrogated me. Mercifully, after what seemed to be seven hours of standing like Gumby at the blackboard, after all the guffaws and twitters had died down, and I was finally back at my desk, Mrs. Retchit would say sweetly, "Surely someone can solve this simple little problem? What about it, Jackie? You can do this in a flash, am I right?" She was always right.

I had trouble throughout my school years with misguided teachers, but my time with Mrs. Retchit was the worst. She instilled in me a total fear of learning. She taught me that learning was not safe. I now had two problems: fear of learning and overload. I don't know which one influenced my school experience more.

It was not a question of intelligence. My IQ was above average, and in circumstances where fear and distractions did not overcome me, I enjoyed learning. I looked for opportunities to be alone in a quiet place with a book on any subject from space exploration to wildlife. But I found it increasingly difficult to pay attention to what was going on in the classroom. My mind was always in overdrive. My fantasies revolved around any and every outside character and prop from a stray dog ambling across the playground to the sound of milkman Hansen's truck, from Mrs. Ackley out for a walk to the empty ball field waiting to be played on.

I was never able to answer my parents' questions as to why I did the things the teachers said I did, or why I didn't do the things they wanted me to do. There must have been a thousand comments from teachers such as, "David doesn't complete his assignments." "David is bright, but he doesn't apply himself." "David just does not pay attention." "David will have to repeat this grade if he does not do better." "David does not try; he is lazy." "David is the class clown." Well, sure, I was the class clown and I was proud of it. I put a lot of work into distracting others and I liked being recognized for what I was rather than for what I was not.

Math was the worst. I didn't see numbers the same way everyone else did. Give me words any day. I never got the hang of putting those blobby little numbers together to come up with something that made sense. It was like trying to arrange stars in some kind of neat, tidy paint-by-number package. I couldn't concentrate long enough to follow a problem through all the steps to its conclusion. I especially hated those stupid story problems. By the time I had read three sentences chock-full of apples and oranges, I had forgotten the first sentence.

I don't blame most of the teachers or my parents or schoolmates for my problems in school. After all, they couldn't experience my situation, so how could they know how it felt? I longed to do what was expected of me, to be able to work along with the class on projects and assignments, to pay attention, to learn. More than anything else I wanted to succeed and belong. And God knows I wanted to break my pattern of rushing through the present routine. I just didn't know how.

By the time I entered high school I was convinced there was something seriously wrong with me, although deep down I knew I was not stupid. I felt deadened by the "I can't do it" that permeated my head and my gut. Echoes of doubt reverberated with each word I spoke each time I thought maybe I had something to say, but at the same time I was getting more and more adept at hiding my shame.

As I reached adolescence the homework battles were getting worse. My mental defenses snapped to red alert status even at the thought of my dad helping me. His participation as substitute teacher was always short-lived. If I failed to grasp an "easy" equation he was so plainly pointing out, he lost his patience—what little he had—and stomped out of the room, leaving a trail of expletives in his wake. Gentle, patient Mom would then come to my rescue until I either grasped it or faked it. "Fake it until you make it" became my tried and trusted motto.

As I reached adolescence I became fussier about my clothes, I experienced more mood swings, and my problems with attention, concentration, frustration tolerance, and memory got worse. I would have a fit if my pants were too tight or too loose. I know all kids go through a thing about clothes, but my reasons were different. Sure, I wanted to look good because it would help me feel better, but there was more to it than that. My reaction to ill-fitting jeans was like my reaction to crowds of people or to being hugged or touched. I felt invaded and violated when I was in too close quarters with anything. I needed my space.

I had learned years before that I could find places of retreat that would afford me some relief from overstimulation and confusion. The first place I found was the hidey-hole under the steps to the basement. It was a great fort and a perfect refuge. The coal bin was a favorite place, too, because it smelled good.

I needed order. I needed to make sense of the world. When I couldn't trust my own thinking or when my surroundings became too chaotic, I sought stability through my touchstone people—my mother and my brother—or in retreat places or through fantasies of an upcoming holiday, weekend, or dinner. Probably because the present was always fleeting and indecipherable, I learned to live for times in the future that offered recreation, retreat, and release: weekends, holidays, summers, any time I could be free of the restraints of school or work. Conjuring up positive feelings about the future helped me cope with the present.

Aside from these coping strategies, I developed three other sources of comfort: music, tobacco, and alcohol. Singing along with Elvis, Little Richard, and the Everly Brothers allowed me to enjoy the fantasy of being someone else for a while. Music flooded me with comfort and made soothing connections among the neurons in my brain.

**The Fly on the Wall**

I discovered tobacco in early adolescence. Those were the days when everyone smoked as if it was the right thing to do. I learned to swing a golf club at age two, and by the age of ten I was regularly trooping around the nine-hole course with other kids. I soon knew all the prime places on the course to smoke where we would not be discovered. We stashed our smokes along the route of the three or so holes that were the most isolated on the course. I could never get enough of those cigarettes. When I learned to inhale I learned to relax. Smokes and I were going to be buddies for many years.

But I didn't really learn the meaning of the word relax until I met the Big A: alcohol. I already had helped Dad finish off a beer now and then and secretly drained quite a few Hamm's or Schlitz cans. The taste was pleasant, but the real message of this elixir didn't reach me until I was around twelve or thirteen. And what better place than the good old golf course to experience that magic moment?

Four of us, including my brother, pilfered several six-packs of beer. Dan and I brought most of it because our dad had the biggest supply and would not notice any missing. We met at the eighth hole to conduct this rite of passage. I really had no premonition that the ceremony would be so memorable. I just thought we would get together to have some smokes and beer, kind of like the big folks did at the VFW.

While I was drinking about the third beer my brain got very excited. It sent me the message that this was the stuff I had been searching for all my life:

Brain to the rest of Dave: "Did you feel what I just felt, ol' buddy?"

"Yeah, what in the hell was that?"

"That, my dear boy, was the nectar of the gods running through us like a healing stream and taking all of our tensions away."

"Yeah, Brain, that's what it feels like all right. Kind of like I've been washed clean of all that ails me."

"You got it, my friend, and we need it. This is the only stuff in the world that will help us swat that fly off the wall down the hall that's been driving us crazy. May you truly relish this magic nectar all your days."

The sense of relief those beers brought was a revelation. I felt free for the first time in my life. Free of the burden of overload. In control. I suddenly could think clearly, unimpeded by the jagged thoughts and feelings that had always cluttered my mind. I knew this was *now!* I was *in* this instant of time, *loving* this instant of time, *never* wanting it to go away. The present had always been my enemy. Now it was my friend. Where had alcohol been all my life? Welcome, beer. Welcome home, Dave.

Of course, I know now that from that first glorious moment I was on my way to the drinker's hall of shame, but I wouldn't discover that until much later. At the time all I knew was that alcohol would be a part of everything important in my life. From learning to working to socializing to sex, alcohol would enable me to be *me* deep down, below all the turmoil and confusion.

Alcohol was my ticket for space travel. From the very first beer several transformations occurred: I was reunited with those parts of me that wouldn't have anything to do with me most of the time, those self-sparkles telling me I'm Cool Dave who could talk intelligently to the opposite sex, or Scholastic Dave who had the right pieces after all to all those mazes of schoolwork riddles, or Singer Dave who was the artist of the song he was now singing.

All the "nots" of who I wasn't or couldn't be seemed to vanish and I felt I was strong and vital, able to be whoever I wanted to be. I had discovered that magic stream of esteem that put me back together again. It was my friend, my lover, a special companion. I could always rely upon it for better feelings than I had. I could simply go to the store on weekends and buy some new feelings. Talk about bottled-up feelings! Well, these really were.

During the next few years, I stumbled through the typical "sow your wild oats" experiences, getting into trouble on some occasions but nothing too serious. My tolerance was so high I could drink a lot and usually make it home without too much trouble. I developed friendships in high school based on drinking on the weekends. If people were not interested in alcohol, I was not interested in them. That easy.

Fishing vacations with my father enabled me to further shape my life around alcohol. He didn't know it, but Dan and I put our devious little minds together, and even before we arrived at our campsite, we knew how we would pilfer the alcohol and cigarettes necessary to ensure a comfortable stay. So I learned at thirteen years of age how to make it in the wilds of Canada on mostly alcohol and cigarettes. These jaunts were actually planned by Dad, so it was not unusual for there to be more alcohol available than food. If for some reason we were to be stuck there in that primitive place, starving would come fast. But it would be painless.

Happy experiences were reinforcing my need to use alcohol. They provided me with the masculine sense of who I was. I was a man doing man things, and it felt good. All the benefits I received from using alcohol could be justified by the societal values of that time and place. But even if that were not true, I received the chemical payoff, relief from my sentrylike vigilance. Relieved of duty.

I was learning a basic lesson. I could live with myself, get along better with myself, as long as I could drink. I could even endure the agony of school during the week if I could look forward to weekends of escape with my tried-and-true friend.

Upon my just-made-it-by-a-thread graduation, all I wanted to do was get as far away from my town as possible. A geographic cure seemed the best thing at the time. You would think that after taking all the scholastic guff I had taken in school, I would certainly not press my luck and go on to college. I really didn't want to go but, according to my parents and the parents of my friends, it was the right thing to do.

So here I was a college joe. It was great until playing the "let's pretend Dave can really do this" game began to be overcome by reality. The realization began to sink in that studying was part of this deal. The novelty of this big-time college experience was wearing off fast. And here they were: old buddy alcohol and some more buddies who also believed in drinking. Let's get it on!

Cutting classes eventually became too easy. School was not going to get in the way of my feeling better. If I could have received college credit for billiards, I would have had an advanced degree. The pool hall had all the right ingredients for stress relief: It was kind of dark, alcohol was served, and the people there knew my name—a regular Cheers kind of place.

After a year of this college game I stopped wasting my parents' money and quit. I had bigger dreams anyway. I entered the military. By the time I enlisted, I was an oblivion-motivated beer drinker on a binge drinking schedule. My military experience was and is a blur. The first morning of basic training in San Antonio confirmed my need for alcohol. After having retired at two in the morning, I was awakened at about four when the drill instructor stomped into the barracks, turned on what must have served as interrogation lighting in World War II, and yelled at the top of his lungs, "Get up, dummies. Your new papa welcomes you."

I had to endure several weeks of this before my exploding nervous system could finally find relief at the nearest bar. For three years, seven months, fourteen days, and seven hours of military duty, I basked in the subcultural acceptance of the drinking man's world. It was not only all right to drink in the service, it was expected. Finally a world that appreciated the dedicated drinking man. If the military expected me to drink, then I was going to do it right. I didn't want to disappoint anyone.

There are many holes in my military memories; probably because my drinking escalated so much that I began to experience blackouts. So my memory, and thus my reality, became even more fragmented than it usually was. I still held a strong belief that alcohol was my friend and my comfort. On many occasions, I drank every moment of my time off and dragged back to duty physically and psychologically spent. I had a series of unpleasant experiences, such as a DUI arrest, losing my car while experiencing a blackout, serious alcohol-related dental problems, and passing out in inappropriate places. (Of course, there is no appropriate place to pass out.) And still, despite the painful consequences, I clung to the soothing comfort alcohol provided. For a while the pleasure of drinking far outweighed the pain.

For a long time, denial and delusion kept me secure in the belief that alcohol was my friend and made my life better. I never considered the possibility that it was causing me problems along with the benefits, at least not long enough to make any serious attempt to quit. I never thought that I might be an alcoholic. Alcoholics were people who couldn't handle their liquor. That wasn't me. Any problems I had because of my drinking I attributed to some other cause or believed were one-time-only occurrences.

Soon after discharge, I met the woman who would become and continues to be my best friend and loving mate, the primary touchstone in my life. Merlene was able, even through the haze of my overload problems and my alcoholism, to see the real me. She recognized that I was at war with the environment, but she saw that I had an eye for its beauty as well.

My first serious attempt to control my drinking came about after a careless accident. I fell asleep with a lit cigarette in my hand following an evening of drinking while visiting my parents. I caught the bed on fire and could have burned down the house if my mother had not smelled the smoke and put out the fire. I was sick from the shame and horror of what I had done and made my first attempt at abstinence. The turmoil I felt was a result of the clash between what my drinking was causing and my need to drink for comfort. The fear of losing my friend and support, alcohol, was strong, but I could no longer convince myself that I could drink with no problem. The resolve to never drink again was strong, almost as strong as the fear of never drinking again. That's when Merlene and I chose to get married. We were both in denial about the seriousness of my problem—I because I needed to believe I was not an alcoholic and could just stop and she because she knew so little about alcoholism that she thought withdrawal was speaking with a southern accent.

Although the excitement of the wedding and finding a house and getting to know my new sons distracted me from the need to drink for a while, my need to drink didn't just disappear. Eventually the pain of abstinence began to escalate. My stress level was high, my tolerance for kid noise very low. My hypersensitivity seemed to lower its boom all at once, and again I turned to that substance I had always been able to trust for relief, alcohol. I told myself it was my reward for being what I considered stepfather of the year. And reward it was. The relief of having a few beers once in a while was so immense that I told myself I could handle drinking now and total abstinence wasn't necessary. Nothing wrong with drinking in moderation.

It became harder and harder to stop when I drank and the consequences were becoming more and more painful. Every time my drinking created problems I would promise my family it would never happen again—I really did mean it—and for a while I would keep my promise. But I had never really learned to function productively without alcohol, and I didn't know how to start. I could go several days, sometimes weeks, without drinking and then, after accumulating so many layers of stress, I would head for a binge.

My drinking as well as my ADHD were making it difficult to make a living. When I was sober, my hypersensitivity interfered with my ability to stick with a job; and when I was drinking, my drinking interfered with my ability to keep a job. I tried factory work. At the can company, noise deflection was a prerequisite for work with cans, cans, and more cans rattling, clanging, banging. (From this moment forward, I vowed to turn over a new leaf. No more cans of beer for me. No sir, just bottles.) I was able to tolerate it by drinking on the job, but needless to say, the job didn't last long.

I tried working for a roofing company; I can't clearly remember what happened to that job. And then finally my dream job came along. I was now going to be a truck drivin' man. I was moving furniture over the road from point A to point Z and loving it. I loved it for about two weeks. My employer, as weird as it seemed at the time, did not see the logic in the beer-stocked cooler that accompanied me on all my trips. He didn't quite buy my idea that beer actually made me a better driver.

Merlene was no longer believing in my promises to quit. She thought I was an alcoholic! I could see how much pain I was causing her. After months and months of drinking, having problems, and swearing off of it, I came face to face with the startling realization that times with my best buddy, alcohol, were about over. The pain of my drinking was about as bad as the pain of not drinking and I couldn't live in between anymore.

They told me at the AA meetings that since I had made a commitment to sobriety, my life would be better than it ever had been. After some early physical discomfort, this seemed to be true. But then it happened. Not all at once, kind of gradually. I fought it with all my strength, but eventually I had to face reality: The fly on the wall down the hall was back and now it was wearing boots!

Overload had returned in full force after a long sleep beneath the covers of alcoholic chemistry. Traffic was louder, voices more invasive, everything more confusing. My stress tolerance was decreasing, my concentration sank to an all-time low, and I was forgetting in seconds all the bits and pieces of information I was expected to remember. I was feeling high levels of stress for no apparent reason. I found myself yelling, slamming doors (my specialty), and resenting telephones and doorbells.

Sensitivity to my environment was both a blessing and a curse. On the one hand, caring and empathy grew out of my heightened awareness of others. But on the other hand, when the volume went up, all I could think of was self-preservation. With every part of me I wanted to push the mess of my world aside and run. I wanted to escape from responsibility, feeling, and especially from giving anything emotionally to anyone else. I tended to retreat into isolation. I would go off by myself without telling anyone what was going on with me. I *couldn't* tell anyone; I didn't know.

Isolating myself from my family often created more problems than it solved. My sobriety was allowing me to see how important my wife and stepchildren were to me. But the children were hearing-impaired and tended to turn up the volume of the environment when I needed it turned down. To stay in the same room with them when I was feeling overwhelmed by my environment, especially if they were talking or playing music, was quite an undertaking. But I knew I couldn't always expect others to adjust to my needs, and I couldn't live in isolation.

Shopping malls were the bane of my existence. On numerous

mall excursions I must have appeared to onlookers as a man possessed by demons as the crowds and cacophony squeezed me out any available exit. Without alcohol to wash away the sharpness of life there seemed no escape from the battering world. If this is sobriety, I thought in despair, who needs it?

I would like to tell you that, in spite of all this, I stayed sober after my commitment to recovery. But I didn't. I relapsed several times. I didn't realize that abstinence-based symptoms of alcoholism that affect thinking and emotions and behavior are very common in recovery. I thought there was a character defect in me that stood in my way of a comfortable sobriety. I didn't have professional treatment and even if I had, no one would have told me I had attention deficit hyperactivity disorder (at that time no one yet realized that adults can have it) or what to do about it. So there were a few times, during the first year, when I didn't hold on, and I drank. Fortunately, my relapses were short and infrequent. I valued my sobriety and the life I had without drinking. And I deeply regretted the times I jeopardized that life for quick but short-lived relief.

Overwhelmed by overload again, though, I knew I had only two options: return to alcohol or find a way to handle my problem. I knew it was not a real choice. Drinking again would take away everything I cared about. The price was too high. So I hung on, and little by little I learned what reduced my overload symptoms and what aggravated them. Through trials and many errors I found that excessive caffeine, too much sugar, hunger, and crowds aggravated my overload network. By eliminating or moderating these things and other stressful situations, I was able to reduce my sensitivity.

I learned the importance of getting plenty of rest, eating regular meals, exercising daily, and scheduling my activities to eliminate as much pressure as possible. I learned to isolate and insulate myself from traffic noise, crowds, power drills and jackhammers, and people eating potato chips or crunching apples. I learned to ask for what I needed from my family and we learned to compromise. What it boiled down to was that anything I could do to improve my internal biochemistry or smooth out or soften my environment reduced the symptoms of my overload.

### The Fly on the Wall

I was taking care of the attention deficit hyperactivity disorder I didn't know I had while telling myself I was protecting myself from the abstinence-based symptoms of my addiction. But regardless of what I called these symptoms, I was learning ways to reduce the severity of them, enabling me to live more comfortably and productively. I was even able to go to college and graduate.

Not that there weren't problems. Of course there were! I was a recovering alcoholic with attention deficit hyperactivity disorder. While I knew very well I was a recovering alcoholic, I was not aware that I had ADHD. But what I did to support my recovery from addiction helped me cope with my ADHD.

My old faithful motto, *fake it until you make it*, helped me survive. Over the years this motto became part of who I was. Over time I learned to cope, and faking it became a way of life. Through childhood, adolescence, young adulthood, and adulthood it helped me and it hurt me. At times it saved me by helping me avoid things I needed to avoid, that I wasn't ready to face. Sometimes it hurt me by keeping me from activities that could have brought pleasure and enriched my life. It led me to use alcohol as an escape, to pretend that everything was all right. It went with me to college and allowed me to bluff my way through for a while. It helped me survive the military. It enabled me to be the clown. I could laugh and make others laugh. It enabled me to bury the part of me that made life unbearable. It helped me put one foot in front of the other when I didn't know what was ahead. But at the same time, it kept me from seeing that there was something wrong in my life that needed to be addressed.

And that something didn't go away when I escaped with alcohol, when I joined the Air Force, when I married and accepted the responsibility of a family. And becoming a counselor to help ease the pain of others didn't fix it either.

Over the years I became weary of faking it. In a vague, nagging way, I knew that many of my problems were connected, but I didn't know precisely how. When I became a counselor and observed people with ADHD, I saw similarities between their experiences and mine. As new research verified that ADHD—with or without hyperactivity—often continues into adulthood, I felt a strong need for an official diagnosis. So I took the big step and arranged for diagnostic interviews and testing at a well-known clinic.

Sure enough, I was diagnosed as having ADHD. It was scary, but I felt like shouting for joy. It was deliverance to know that I was not suffering from a personality defect or a lack of moral fiber. My attacker had a face and a name: Attention Deficit Hyperactivity Disorder. It was a start at knowing what I could change and what I couldn't. It was something I could learn about and apply that knowledge to living more productively. I also knew it was not going to kill me. Instead of my life flying apart as I attempted to find reasons for my problems, I could now apply myself within the restricted but liberating context of truth my diagnosis gave me. The journey would be lifelong, but now I could get on with the journey. I could go forward instead of going one step ahead and two back.

Accepting the reality of what I have has enabled me to take better care of myself. I have learned to give myself permission to do what is important for my recovery from ADHD as well as for my recovery from addiction. I have learned to live rather than escape life. My disorder has not been cured, but I have learned to control the symptoms. The storm waves in my life have quieted; the harshness has softened; the jagged edges have been smoothed; my torment has ceased. The fly on the wall down the hall is still there but it is no longer driving me crazy.

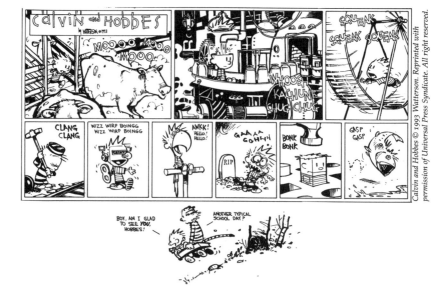

# 2

## Attention Deficit Hyperactivity Disorder

It is usually with a great sense of relief that the diagnosis of attention deficit disorder is received. It is not that people are happy to have the condition; but already aware that something is very wrong in their lives, they are relieved to know they have something specific that can be acknowledged and treated. And the awareness that it is primarily a physical condition rather than a character defect brings the reassurance that they are not to blame.

While it is true that only a few years ago few people had heard of attention deficit hyperactivity disorder, today it is the most common behavioral disorder in American children (5 to 7 percent of school-age children have been diagnosed). It has become the subject of thousands of studies and symposiums and is fraught with much controversy.

ADHD has three main hallmarks: extreme distractibility, an almost reckless impulsiveness, and—in some cases but not all—a knee-jerking, toe-tapping hyperactivity that makes sitting still all but impossible. This gives us some clue to the excitable nature of the victim's brain state. Indeed, with ADHD, a ticking clock or sounds and sights caught through a window can drown out a teacher's voice. People with ADHD act before thinking; they are unable to wait their turn and find it difficult to play by the rules.

Once thought to be a childhood behavior problem, ADHD is actually a genetic disorder that affects brain chemistry and is passed from one generation to the next.[1] Once believed to disappear in adolescence, it is now known to continue into adulthood. Since it is passed from parent to child, in many families both the parent *and* child may have the condition, creating a unique and confusing family dysfunction.

Attention deficit disorder is baffling and distressing not only for the children and adults who experience it but also for family members, teachers, friends, and coworkers. Children with the condition may be intelligent and creative but do poorly in school. Adults may be motivated to succeed but flit from job to job. Children or adults may be caring and sensitive but give the impression they have no interest in what others are experiencing.

While there is a wide variety of ADHD symptoms, not everyone with the condition has the same symptoms. Two people may have similar symptoms but react to them differently. Children and adults may have different ways of coping with the same problems. The condition is not all-or-nothing. Some people have fewer symptoms and/or experience them less intensely, while others experience the symptoms so severely that their lives are totally dysfunctional.

Even "normal" people have *some* ADHD-like symptoms, at least occasionally. The difference between this and the ADHD person is that for adults or children with attention deficit hyperactivity disorder, it is not a matter of symptoms that come and go but rather an ongoing, *always-present* state or condition from which they get little relief. Their personalities become defined by the symptoms.

Many of the symptoms of attention deficit hyperactivity disorder are a reflection of a common underlying problem: a heightened awareness of sights, sounds, touch, taste, and smells. All incoming stimuli are so powerful that unwanted or insignificant signals cannot be filtered out of awareness. Result: Overload, a feeling of being bombarded by the environment, making it impossible to concentrate on a single idea or plan for any length of time. Along with this condition—and often a result of it—the person with attention deficit hyperactivity disorder will usually experience a variety of other symptoms.

## Common Symptoms

There are two general types of attention deficit hyperactivity disorder. Some people have one type or the other but many have both. One type is primarily characterized by inattention, the other by hyperactivity and impulsivity.[2] The term currently being applied to the condition by professionals reflects these two types of symptoms: *attention deficit/hyperactivity disorder* (AD/HD).

Contrary to early thinking, not all people with this condition exhibit hyperactivity. Although hyperactivity was the first symptom to be identified, it has become apparent that many people suffering from the condition are not hyperactive. Many people who do not exhibit external hyperactivity experience an internal hyperactivity—a sense of urgency, a feeling of being driven, or a constant need to hurry (even when there's no reason). People who are not *typically* hyperactive are less likely to be recognized as having the condition and less apt to get the help they need than the obviously hyperactive person. Nor does everyone who is hyperactive have the symptoms of inattention. As we look at some of the symptoms, remember that the condition varies a great deal from one person to another and a person may have either type or both types and different symptoms and manifestations of either type.

### Difficulty Focusing Attention[3]

Perhaps the most common problem connected with attention deficit hyperactivity disorder is distractibility. A short—although sometimes extraordinarily intense—attention span is characteristic and can severely impair a person's ability to function. Both adults and children with this symptom have difficulty concentrating regardless of the importance of the task or situation facing them.

> Tim: *It's hard for me to stay on track. I just get overwhelmed. I think about way too many things at the same time. I just can't get through college. When I go from one class to another class, by the time I reach the third class of the day my mind is still not only on the first class but on tomorrow and last night. Is one of my socks inside out? Stuff like that.*

Attentional deficit children have a shorter attention span than other children the same age. Adults with the condition are unable to concentrate on an immediate task because they are distracted by even insignificant stimuli. Children are often told by parents and teachers that they do not listen. Adults frequently hear the same accusation from a spouse, friend, or coworker.

Not everyone experiences distractibility the same way. It may appear in girls differently than in boys. Girls may be accused of day-dreaming or "spacing out" while boys may be going rapidly from one focus of attention to another. But either way, they are not focusing on what they are expected to focus on.

### Difficulty Organizing Tasks[4]

The thinking and behavior of people with an attention deficit is often disorganized and chaotic. Wanting and needing organization without knowing how to get it, they are dependent on others to provide it. If this help is not available, the result is likely to be confusion and disorganization.

> Barb: *I decided to record some of my thoughts about having attention deficit disorder. When I was ready to record, after I had written some things down, it took me a while just to get the tape recorder. I couldn't remember where it was. I found it in the closet, but the closet was so disorganized I had a hard time getting it out. When I got it out I had to find the record button because machines intimidate me. I pushed the record button, but it didn't record. I finally figured out you have to push "record" and "play" at the same time. Great, it's working. But then I realized a tape was in the recorder that I shouldn't be recording over. I needed a different tape. When I tried to tape on the new tape, it wouldn't work. Which then just triggered all my shame about being no good with technical equipment. It's almost as if a spirit of paranoia takes over—that something or somebody is messing with me. It just triggered all kinds of feelings. I ended up pounding on the record button and broke it! So then I had to get my sister's recorder and go through some more headaches just to tape. It's kind of funny now but it wasn't at the time.*

Some projects are never begun because of the inability to organize the steps necessary to get started. Other tasks are started but not completed because, unable to see how parts go together to make a whole, the person simply cannot figure out what to do next. Some of this may be overlooked in a child as a sign of immaturity. But an adult who is unable to set priorities or to figure out what job needs to be done next is likely to have endless problems.

Mary settled for a job as waitress even though her education qualified her for a variety of other positions. When it came right down to it, she couldn't face the stress she anticipated in a job where she would have to make decisions, organize projects, and meet deadlines.

Another reason that some people are unable to organize tasks is a distorted perception of time and space. This may include impaired discrimination of size, poor spatial orientation, and an inability to judge distance or time. An amusing incident with one ADHD child occurred when she heard her dad say, "That clock is fast." She responded with, "If you think that clock is fast, you should see the clock in the lunchroom at school. It's so fast sometimes I don't have time to finish my lunch."

People with ADHD feel confused much of the time by lack of an internal road map. They don't have a sense of direction, sometimes not even a sense of right and left. They easily become disoriented about how to get from one place to another and find this very embarrassing.

Lyn: *I have a real problem with getting lost. I get confused and can't remember where to go even though I have been there before. I have learned different ways to cope with that today, but it still happens. Perhaps I'm going to the dentist—something very stressful for me. I might have gone to that dentist for years and then one day I get confused: Is his office at First and Market or Second and Main. I get more and more anxious and then I can't find it. I clutch up and everything gets disoriented.*

*Back in kindergarten it was a big deal to take the little wagon and go get milk for the class. One day I got picked to go get the milk. At first I was real happy. Then as I stepped into the hallway with the wagon I was—well, I don't think to say I was terrorized is an exaggeration. Suddenly I was completely lost. I stood out in the hallway with that empty wagon and the hall looked so long and so dark. I felt stupid and I was embarrassed. I feel sad now when I recall it.*

*When I was a teenager and started to drink there was an explanation for it. If you are drunk you are expected to get turned around. That's something that has persisted through my recovery to this day. If I get stressed I get confused.*

Jon says that his hunting buddies always put him along the river when they do a deer drive because when he is supposed to walk through the timber they spend the whole day looking for him instead of hunting deer. Many people can go easily from one place to another if they know the route or have specific directions but do not have a sense of where they are in relation to where they are going. Carl feels that other people seem to have a map in their heads so they have a general sense of where one place is in relationship to another. "I don't have a map like that," he says. "If I don't know exactly how to go to get somewhere, I can't figure it out."

**The Way Home**
by David

Did it again!
Drove off the end of the world it seemed,
fighting myself, fear laced heavily with anger—
rage at the injustice of it all.
Why can't I ever find my way?
Why can't I?
Why?

Driving faster—a fit soul-deep shoving me—
frantic, searching for a home, for belonging,
simply for a way into familiar connections,
a way out of mad.
Mind charged with prickly particles,
negative energy driving itself into circular confusion—
cornered animal frenzy.

The time bandit steals my power,
once again trashing my lunch date, myself.
I'm detached now and fatigued,
my energy spent once again fighting myself.
Now floating in space, I try to find a marker,
a lifeline where I can attach to being
and find the light illuminating my way home.

## Difficulty Following Tasks through to Completion[5]

Life for people with attentional deficits may consist of a series of uncompleted tasks. Or the problem may show up as a pattern of broken promises or commitments. A child starts to put together a kite and never finishes it. An adult never finishes balancing the checkbook.

> Robin: *The most frustrating part of my ADD is the frustration of never really accomplishing what I set out to accomplish. Bridges burned behind me and bridges under construction in front of me that probably will not be finished by the time I need to cross them. Goals never accomplished. Nothing concrete where I can say yeah I completed this or accomplished that. I can't even learn from what I do accomplish or what I don't accomplish.*

A sincere interest or commitment may fade rapidly as a new interest or commitment takes its place. First the family, then the teacher, then the employer, and eventually the community may simply give up on the person with this problem because trust has been violated too often. The person may not only disappoint others but disappoint him- or herself.

> Brian: *It always made me mad that I couldn't keep a journal. I started many times to write, but then I would forget where it was or just forget to do it. A daily routine was no routine.*

People with an attention deficit are likely to have an attic full of projects started and never finished; a file drawer full of great plans never undertaken. Adults have frequent financial problems caused by their failure to pay bills on time or legal snarls because they did not take care of problems as they arose.

## Hyperactivity[6]

> Phyllis: *When my son was in the third grade, he would have times when he just went ballistic. I can't think of any other way to describe it. Just like a little tornado. I wanted him to stop and I kept putting him on his bed, saying, "You cannot do this. You have to stop." He'd get up and I'd put him back. I swatted him on the butt and I hit him several*

*times. Mostly, I remember the struggle of trying to get him to be still and not tear things up. He was just off. And I think that was because he got so hyperstimulated, and so uncomfortable inside his own body, that he didn't know what to do. He just went off.*

People with hyperactivity are always moving. From early childhood they are bundles of energy. As babies and very young children they are squirmy, cranky, and "into everything." School-age children cannot sit still; they fidget and fiddle with everything in sight. A child may respond to a request to "leave the book alone" only to pick it up again in five minutes.

Anne: *It's hard on any kid with hyperactivity. But in some ways it's harder for a girl. A guy is supposed to be full of energy. He's just being a boy. But I was raised that girls were supposed to be quiet. They were supposed to play quietly—to do quiet things with dolls and paper dolls. My neighbor used to cut the Betsy McCall dolls out of the paper for me to play with. I'd go to her house and she would have them all cut out and she'd be ready to play paper dolls with me. But I didn't want to. I wanted her attention and approval, but I didn't know how to play paper dolls. I didn't know how to sit and do that. Just folding the paper edges over the stand-up dolls was extremely frustrating for me.*

Sometimes hyperactivity seems to disappear as a person grows older, leading to the belief that the ADHD has gone away when only this major symptom has diminished. Other symptoms, then, are left unaddressed because the person is no longer obviously hyperactive. Most adults learn to restrain their hyperactivity so they are less disruptive, but they may still be restless and always on the go. They may pace while talking on the phone or find it very difficult to sit for an hour to listen to a lecture or sermon. If they can't avoid such a situation, they continually change position, doodle, or shuffle their feet.

Terry: *All my life my mother told me, "You don't know when to stop." But I didn't know how to stop. I didn't have an off button. I would pester my brother, and as I did, the momentum would build and it would become a frenzy. I couldn't stop. I knew I was going to get in trouble, but I couldn't turn it off. There were no brakes at all in my behaviors. It caused a lot of pain and frustration for my family and a lot of shame for me. I couldn't understand why I couldn't do it. Even when I was married, Pat would tell me, "You just don't know when to quit." I'm a natural risk taker. I like to take risks—to try new things. It's as if going to new places and starting new projects helps me use up some of the energy that tends to be free-floating inside me.*

## Inability to Wait[7]

One ADHD symptom that is almost universal is impatience. Children with the disorder can't tolerate delays and have difficulty waiting their turn. In the cafeteria line or in line to buy movie tickets, they fidget and jostle and grumble.

Adults experience this symptom as feeling always in a hurry, even when there is no reason. They feel edgy waiting for a bus, standing in line at the bank, or waiting for traffic lights to turn green. Even if they also have symptoms of inattention and are distracted easily, they often experience a sense of urgency when they're involved in a task and feel driven to keep moving ahead.

People with ADHD are seldom content in the present. They feel driven to hurry through whatever is going on in order to get on to the next thing. Like Joseph who after his first day of kindergarten asked if he was going to first grade tomorrow, they feel compelled to get on with getting on. It is as though the present is their enemy. Always reaching out for a reality that eludes their grasp, they feel a constant frustration and internal anguish they have no words to describe.

*Randy: I have never been satisfied with where I am. I am always looking ahead for the next activity like I was going to get happiness there. I used to drive people nuts. We'd go from one party to another party to another. They'd say, "Why don't we just chill out and hang around here." I'd say, "No, no. There's another party going on down the road and we need to get there."*

*It's been the same with jobs. I've always left for a place that was better. I had one job, though, that really fit my ADD. Route salesman for Coca-Cola. I could go from one place to another. At first I had trouble learning the route because I have a direction problem. But once I figured out where I was supposed to go and when, it was great. I was always able to do what I came to do quickly and be off to the next place. That's me. Always off to the next place or next activity.*

## Impulsiveness[8]

Children and adults with ADHD may be impatient and impulsive, often disregarding the long-term consequences of their behavior. They are so focused on immediate gratification and momentary rewards that they often put themselves and those around them in danger. Without stopping to think, they take unnecessary risks. As children they may dash into the street without looking, jump out of trees, hit other children with slight provocation, or get carried away and play too rough. They seem to wonder "what would happen if—" and take risks without thinking through the consequences.

> Joe: *When I was young I lived near a river with cliffs. There is a walk bridge that is very dangerous. You can climb up the pillar on the bridge and then jump out over a bunch of brush and cliffs to the river. Although some people have jumped off this cliff, no one had ever dove off it. One day, to show off, I decided on impulse to dive off. I told someone to throw in an inner tube as soon as I hit the water because I didn't know what kind of shape I would be in when I came up. I knew I could be badly hurt and I did it anyway.*
>
> *I also did things like jumping trains that were going under the railroad bridge. If you didn't have your timing right, you could land between the cars and fall onto the tracks.*

Adults may make decisions that affect their entire lives without considering the long-term consequences. Adults plagued by impulsive behavior may make snap decisions, blurt out things they are sorry for later, and do things that to others seem reckless. They may drive too fast or too aggressively, take reckless chances in sports, or use power tools without recommended safeguards. They are usually poor planners and take off in several directions at once. They may quit jobs, walk out of important meetings, or create financial problems with impulse buying.

Morgan: *The difficulties I have today in my life are difficulties with setting priorities and organizing my time. I'm impulsive and get too busy with things that really are not that important. I say yes without thinking and have difficulty planning because I take on too much. And all this together affects my self-esteem. I have to work continually to try to make these obstacles easier to deal with so I don't feel so bad about myself.*

*I have always done impulsive things that I have no explanation for. One summer when I was about five, my sister—who loved to read— decided she was going to read to me. We were lying on a blanket out in the yard. My sister was lying on her side with her head propped up by her arm. She read on and on and I got so bored listening to her voice that I reached over and knocked her arm out from under her. Her head fell down and hit the ground. Suddenly I was being screamed at. She was trying to be a good big sister to me and why couldn't I appreciate it? It was like there was something wrong with me because I couldn't lie still and just enjoy listening to her read. But I couldn't explain why I suddenly hit her arm. It was an impulsive act.*

## Symptoms of the Symptoms of ADHD

The primary symptoms of ADHD invariably lead to secondary symptoms that are disruptive to the life of the person with the condition as well as to family members. As life becomes more and more complicated because of impulsive decisions and unfinished tasks, problems pile up on problems. Life is affected physically, psychologically, socially, economically, and spiritually.

### Underachievement

Cindy showed an unusual aptitude for music. She had perfect pitch, a clear and beautiful soprano voice, and a dream of becoming a great musician. But her dream never came true because—though she tried violin, piano, and voice—she never stuck with them beyond the first few lessons because she could not endure the scales and exercises.

ADHD does not affect intelligence. Yet teachers often complain: "He is not working up to his potential." Or, "She is an under-achiever." There are a number of factors that may account for the "underachiever syndrome." It may be due to the inability to sustain attention. People with ADHD also give up easily because they cannot stick with a task that is unpleasant and are unable to tolerate boredom or repetition.

For reasons that are not entirely understood, ADHD children of normal or above intelligence may have a specific area of learning difficulty, usually in reading or math. They may recognize individual words but have trouble putting them together in sentences. They may be able to add columns of numbers quite rapidly but be unable to solve a story math problem. Their inability to concentrate often interferes with completion of math problems that require following a chain of thought from one point to a point far removed.

> Leslie: *There were yellow birds, red birds, and blue birds. The yellow birds were the dodo birds. The red birds were average (you could play with them). And the blue birds were the smart kids. In reading I was a blue bird. I was a red bird in a few things, but I was a yellow bird in math. One of the difficult things about it was that the teachers thought I was doing it on purpose because I was real bright in reading. And anyone who could read that well should be able to do this simple arithmetic if they would just try harder or do the homework. I just couldn't get it. My parents thought I was doing it to get attention. And that felt bad because I really couldn't get it. I just couldn't. In high school I tried very hard in algebra and still got a D. And I flunked geometry. By then my attitude was, "I don't care; it's not my thing. I'm not going to do it."*

## Poor Memory

A natural result of poor concentration is poor memory. It is difficult enough to remember all the ordinary things of daily living, but when we do not or cannot concentrate, the information never really gets implanted in the brain. So, of course, it is difficult or impossible to remember it no matter how important it may be.

Syl: *One time my dad was going to spank me because I had lied to him. He wanted me to tell him what a lie was. He even gave me the defini-tion several times, but I couldn't remember it well enough to recite it back. When my sister came in he asked her to tell me what a lie meant and then asked me to repeat what she said. I couldn't. Even today when my stress levels go up I cannot access my memory or keep a train of thought.*

There may also be other reasons that people with ADHD have trouble remembering. The process of visual imaging may be differ-ent. In the book *Attention Deficit Disorder: A Different Perception*, Thom Hartman had this to say:

When you say to a "normal" person: "Go to the store and pick up a bottle of milk, a loaf of bread, and some orange juice, then stop at the gas station and fill up the car on the way home," the "normal" person will create a mental picture of each of those things as they hear them described. They picture the store, the milk, the bread, the juice, and the gas station. This congruence of verbal and visual images makes for high-quality memory. But an ADHD person may only hear the words without creating the mental pictures so vital to memory.

Becky: *Another way my confidence and self-esteem is battered is by misplacing things. Since it's difficult focusing in any given moment, I have trouble recalling information. When making a sandwich, my mind is getting the bread long before I'm done making the tuna salad. So I can't remember if I put all the ingredients in the tuna salad or not and this happens a lot!*

**Low Frustration Tolerance**

ADHD people tend to have sudden anger outbursts followed by the uncomfortable feeling that they have overreacted. Bombarded by unwanted sensations, they tend to be tense and uptight most of the time. When things do not go the way they hope or when their attempts to escape a stressful situation are blocked, they tend to ex-plode. They may yell, slam doors, break things, or have temper tantrums. Some ADHD adults learn to control their tempers most of the time, with only occasional outbursts. Others continue to lose jobs, get into fights, and destroy relationships because of violent and usually unexpected outbursts.

People often remarked about what a pleasant personality Wayne had. He was well liked by family, friends, and coworkers. He liked people and had a full social life. But on occasion the frustration of living with ADHD was too much for him. For no apparent reason he would explode with anger. These outbursts drained and fatigued him. How did they come on so fast? Why did they occur at all? When Wayne calmed down he could think of nothing that justified his earlier behavior, nothing that explained his yelling and door-slamming. He was always remorseful and vowed it would never happen again, but it always did. When he broke a new and expensive briefcase over a chair, it frightened him so much he got some counseling. He had struggled all his life with these outbursts and he was tired. But no insight he gained from the counseling helped Wayne understand what was behind his anger. He thought for a while he had conquered the problem. Then, when he was least expecting it, another outburst occurred, leaving him more remorseful and confused than ever.

**Ode to Morning**
by David

Ranting, raving, swearing, stewing.
Wonder if you can guess what I am doing.
Probably not.
Unless, of course, it's been your lot
To fight the good fight over a cereal box.

I twist, turn, pull, and pry
This soldered package 'til I nearly cry.
Rage explodes, rips it open.
Bits of wheat, scattered, broken
On the floor, stepped upon.
New problem now at dawn.

Oh me, oh my. What do I do?
Here am I in another stew

Created, shaped, and formed by you—
A stupid box that happens to be
Fused closed and kept from me.

Along with low frustration tolerance, many ADHD people have an inability to tolerate change, especially an unexpected change of plans. For such people, even a minor change in routine can be highly disruptive. A child may get upset because weather disrupts plans for an outing. An adult may get upset if road repairs force a change in the usual route to work. People with this problem may insist upon sticking with a plan even when circumstances change and the plan is no longer the best option.

This inability to tolerate change probably comes from the need in ADHD people to rely on things outside of them because they have come to believe they cannot rely on their own abilities or judgments.

Kim: *When my daughter Allison was five and a half, I remember being called at work. She was in the cafeteria and she refused to leave. By the time I got there, she was in the conference room with the principal and the counselor, crying violently. I told her it was time to go home and she screamed that she wasn't going. It took thirty minutes and at least four attempts to get Allison to the car. She would break away and run back to the school. She tried to jump out of the car twice while it was moving. She was dead set on going back to the school to watch a film she had planned on seeing that they didn't show.*

## Low Self-Esteem

It is not difficult to understand why most people who have ADHD have low self-esteem. They see little that they have accomplished, little that they can feel proud of. They get regular feedback from the people they associate with that they are just not making it. What is there to feel good about?

Kim: *We adopted Allison when she was five days old. I knew by the time she was three that she marched to her own beat. And I liked getting into her world and sharing her perspective. By preschool age, things changed. She was not like the other children and did not have a clue as to how to socialize with them. Allison didn't have a sense of physical or spatial boundaries. When asking kids to play with her she was literally in their face. She would intimidate the children just because she was so close. She would come on very strong. Allison was impulsive and many times aggressive, reacting to the rejection of others. She spent much time at a separate table in time-out. All this was very painful for her and painful for us to watch. She was constantly ostracized at school and would come home crying, saying she hated recess because no one played with her. It just broke my heart.*

## Life Out of Control

People with ADHD often feel that life controls them rather than they control life. While they are attempting to figure out and handle one series of problems, another set comes along and hits them in the head. The old saying, You can't drain the swamp when you're up to your neck in alligators, certainly describes the situation of most people with ADHD.

Brad: *I have an ongoing sense of not being in control of my life. I have no idea what to do with the clutter. Life wears me out. I'm always playing catch-up. I'm always juggling things, never completing anything because something else comes up. My wife says I make extra work for myself because I don't know how to work smart, but I really don't know what that means. She tells me to take care of one thing at a time and to finish it before I start something else. But something urgent always comes up and I shift gears in midstream. I make people mad because I don't do what I say I will. And while I am trying to mend that fence, I let someone else down. So my relationships with people are always shaky no matter what I do. I just don't seem able to cope with the complexities of life. The depressing thing to me is that I know I am capable of doing so much more with my life, but I'm so busy juggling that I never get the things done I really want to do. I see my life passing by with nothing to show for it but my "unfulfilled potential."*

# 3

---

# Causes and Consequences

Now that we have looked at the more observable symptoms of ADHD, it may be useful to look more closely at some underlying conditions that generate or intensify them and the consequences of living with ADHD.

## Overload

While ADHD is usually described by identifying symptoms that *others can see*, an *internal* symptom may be the most powerful and may be even the force behind the observable symptoms. This is an internal dysfunction related to the perception of environmental stimuli. People with ADHD are afflicted with a deficit in the sensory filtering system. The brain normally has the ability to block out irrelevant stimuli. Most people screen out of their awareness the sound of the refrigerator running, distant traffic noise, conversations from across the room or down the hall, or the sound of sparrows chirping in a tree outside the window. They are able to filter out these distractions.

Most people with ADHD cannot. For them these distractions are *augmented* internally—thus the name *stimulus augmentation*. People with this condition hear everything, see everything, feel everything. The world rushes in unfiltered and unimpeded. An unwanted, disorganized flood of information pours in ceaselessly.

> His porous system absorbs instantly all that is in the environment, and the absorption is so fast and intense and pervasive that it "floods" the person.
>
> Lynn Weiss, *Attention Deficit Disorder in Adults*

People with this condition are aware of anything and everything that is happening around them. They seem to be constantly monitoring their environment. Ever vigilant, they notice everything. Conversations unrelated to their own invade them. The sound of another person's chewing is loud and distracting. The trash truck demands as much attention as the boss on the phone. The person with this condition is trapped into devoting so much attention to life's nonessential stimuli that very little attention is left for what is considered important. The whistle of a train six blocks away derails the train of thought needed to solve a math problem or to write a report.

> Henry: *When I am at a business lunch and really need to listen to the conversation, I can only get part of the story because I am trying so hard to shut out the noise of other conversations and distractions in the room. I am aware of meaningless word fragments that come catapulting at me from every direction, of dishes clattering, phones ringing, people moving about. The people with me seem to have a fence around them that protects them from this barrage of noise and activity. I don't have a fence.*

The pervasiveness of stimulus augmentation—affecting thinking, feeling, and behavior—easily explains the presence of the more observable symptoms. Concentration is broken; memory is affected. Stress levels are high, leading to frustration, mood swings, and temper outbursts. The constant assault on the senses leaves people with ADHD weary and fatigued. They have a sense of being bombarded by the world around them, of being battered by life.

## Labels and History

The labels applied to the condition we now refer to as ADHD have varied over the years according to the prevailing beliefs about its symptoms at any certain time. Other than the name itself, there is nothing new about this suddenly ubiquitous disorder. Certainly, the world, as we know it, has had its share of impulsive and obnoxious children and has generally treated them as behavior problems rather than patients. Most of the world still does so: Europe and nations like France and England report one-tenth the U.S. rate of ADHD. In Japan, the disorder has barely been studied.

It was described in children before 1902 as a "defect in moral control" due to failure by these children to control their actions. The historical medical record on ADHD is said to have begun that year when British pediatrician, George Still, published an account of twenty children in his practice who, according to Still, were "passionate," "defiant," "spiteful," and "lacking inhibitory volition." At that time, Still made the remarkable suggestion that "bad parenting was not to blame." Instead he suspected a subtle brain injury. This theory gained credence in the years following the 1917–18 epidemic of viral encephalitis, when it was observed by clinicians that the infection left children with impaired attention, memory, and control over their impulses. By the '40s and '50s the same set of symptoms was called "minimal brain damage."

When it was found that children without known brain injuries had the same characteristics, the label was changed to "minimal brain dysfunction." When hyperactivity was considered the identifying symptom, it was referred to as "hyperkinetic impulse disorder," or simply "hyperactivity." When the condition was found in children who were not hyperactive and the major identifying symptom was the inability to pay attention, the term "attention deficit disorder" was adopted. It was eventually termed "attention deficit hyperactivity disorder," which still implied that everyone so diagnosed had both attentional deficits and hyperactivity.

Very recently, it has been called attention deficit/hyperactivity disorder to reflect the current understanding that there are actually two broad types of symptoms: inattention and hyperactivity—and that it is possible to have one type without having the other. Because of the confusion of when to use which term, we have chosen for use in this book the term "attention deficit hyperactivity disorder" to refer to any form because it is in such common usage that most people easily recognize the terminology. In using this term we recognize that not all people with this condition are hyperactive and not all have the primary symptom of inattention, but that ADHD is a condition that may include any of a number of symptoms.

Over the years, ADHD has been blamed on food additives, viral infections, sugar, lead poisoning, head trauma, and poor parenting. Until recently the search has been primarily for external or environmental causes. Childhood trauma, abuse, and family dysfunction have been suspect. Because so many ADHD sufferers are children of alcoholics it is sometimes assumed that symptoms result from being raised in an alcoholic home. Only recently, as both alcoholism and ADHD have been associated with imbalances in brain chemistry, have defective genes begun to be recognized as a reason for the high incidence of ADHD among children of alcoholics.

## Biological Clues

In 1937, a Rhode Island pediatrician reported that administering stimulants to children with ADHD symptoms had the unexpected effect of calming them down. In the 1990s, the stimulant Ritalin has become the most prescribed drug for this condition. Scientifically, we know that Ritalin works through release of the powerful brain chemical messenger, *dopamine*. In the area of the brain called the *reward center*, dopamine interacts with a family of brain receptors (D1, D2, D3, D4, D5), most profoundly with the D2 type.

However, the vital question was still whether there was indeed a real biological cause of ADHD. As some skeptics put it, "just because something responds to a drug doesn't mean it is a sickness." ADHD researchers counter the skeptics by pointing to a growing body of biological clues. A converging body of evidence from lesion studies in animals and humans, brain imaging studies, EEG studies, responses to medication, and genetic studies supports the premise that ADHD is primarily biologically based.

The precise nature of this biological deficit has remained elusive, although the preponderance of evidence points toward involvement of the frontal-striatal system of the brain. Sophisticated techniques for taking pictures of the brain have supported the theory of abnormal frontal lobe development and function in ADHD.[1] Whether or not this is a *cause* of ADHD we are not in a position to say.

What researchers do say with great certainty is that the condition is inherited. While external factors such as birth injuries or maternal alcohol or nicotine abuse *may* play a role, it can account for less than 10 percent of the ADHD population. But the influence of genes is unmistakable. Russell Barkley of the University of Massachusetts Medical Center estimates that 40 percent of ADHD children have a parent who has the condition.

## The Neurology of ADHD

The case is becoming overwhelmingly strong that there is a physiological cause of ADHD and that attention deficit hyperactivity disorder is a failure in the system of the brain that fine-tunes attention. Chemicals in the brain called neurotransmitters carry messages from one brain cell to another. The availability and balance of neurotransmitters strongly influences our behavior and feelings of well-being.

It was a major breakthrough when scientists discovered that the production and utilization of these neurotransmitters are controlled by our genes. Studies indicate that people with ADHD may have at least one defective gene that makes it difficult for neurons to respond to dopamine, a key neurotransmitter involved in feelings of pleasure and the regulation of attention.

### Reward Deficiency

When there is a deficit in feelings of pleasure because neurotransmitters are not functioning to provide the normal reward feelings of well-being, we have a "reward deficiency." ADHD is a reward deficiency condition. As human beings we are dependent on certain intrinsic and external rewards in order to reinforce certain behaviors and deal with painful situations. We become unconsciously reliant upon our brains and our bodies to provide such reward. But when neurotransmitters are not interacting in a way to produce the good feelings that nature intended, there is a reward deficiency. Instead of the payoffs the brain normally gives us in response to certain ways of thinking and behaving, people with reward deficiency are left with feelings of discomfort, incompleteness, and a yearning for something to help them feel better.

Reward deficiency affects thinking processes, feelings, and corresponding behaviors. It creates a conflictual war with the stuff of life, leaving the afflicted person feeling "too this" or "too that," never just okay. Reward-deficient behaviors may sometimes appear to the onlooker as rather petty or childish. Sometimes others may be totally unaware of the discomfort, as compensating smiles cover it up. But even when one is skilled in hiding feelings, many words and actions are spewed out before one thinks through the consequences. For the sensitive ADHD person, this experience is painful, both physically and mentally.

How do people deal with the conflicts of this reward deficiency day in and day out? They deal with it as best as they can without any instruction or tools for doing so. They compensate and adapt. They may be fearful and angry. They may smile and laugh to hold in the frustrations and tensions. They may look to others to give them what they need—and no one can.

One person experiencing a reward deficiency may savor a quiet time with coffee and newspaper in the morning and anticipate a relaxing game of golf and television viewing in the evening—but wage war with the time in between. Another person may seek to compensate for reward deficiency through activities such as skydiving or a game of racquetball. Using whatever works, a person will look for ways to create that reward when there is a lack of natural feelings of pleasure.

### Brain Waves

Associated with brain chemistry imbalances are abnormal brain wave patterns. Brain waves are the electrical impulses given off by the brain. People with ADHD tend to have abnormal brain waves. Their beta waves (brain waves associated with concentration) are low, and their theta waves (waves associated with drowsiness or daydreaming) are stronger.[2] Of course, everyone experiences all mental states so we cannot say that being in a theta state is only associated with ADHD. But for a person with ADHD it seems to be the normal mental state or the state to which the person automatically reverts. Activities that produce beta waves (problem solving and concentration activities) are difficult for ADHD people to sustain.

Anne: *When I was a Campfire girl I had to do all these crafts. I was always in trouble; I didn't sit quietly. My Campfire leader was teaching us to sew. Everyone else was almost through with the project and I had*

*barely begun. I was sitting there looking out the window. The leader
asked me what I was doing. I told her, "I am thinking about how the
wind feels in my hair when I'm riding my bicycle." Sewing lessons
couldn't hold my attention. That set me apart because everyone else
was content to sit there and sew. They had done it "right." I, again,
had not. The leader told my mom I was the only Campfire girl who
had not completed her project.*

## Associated Conditions

There are a number of conditions that often coexist with attention
deficit hyperactivity disorder. Some of these conditions may result
from ADHD; others may be part of ADHD or due to the same genetic
disorder. But they are all conditions that have been directly linked
with it. A substantial proportion of people with ADHD also have
learning disorders, conduct disorder, antisocial personality disorder,
or Tourette syndrome.

Conduct disorder is a condition often seen along with ADHD that
may be a manifestation of the same genetic condition. The diagnosis
of conduct disorder is made when there is persistent breaking of society's rules and little regard for the rights of others. It includes behaviors such as fighting, lying, and stealing. While not everyone with
conduct disorder can be diagnosed as having ADHD, and certainly
not everyone with ADHD has conduct disorder, they often occur together. It is easy to see why and how someone with ADHD could develop the behaviors of "conduct disorder" and eventually "antisocial
personality disorder" (a condition in adults that includes the same
types of behaviors as conduct disorder).

Tom: *When I was young and the stimulation got too much I would yell
and scream. Once when I was about ten a teacher told me if I didn't learn
to control my anger I was going to be taken away, that the police would
come and arrest me. My anger outburst was the result of an episode in
the classroom when everything became unbearable for me. I tried to
correct it by wiping out the whole classroom. I turned desks over,
knocked things off the teacher's desk, threw chairs across the room.*

By ages five to seven, half to two-thirds of children with ADHD
are hostile and defiant; by age ten to twelve, they are at risk of devel-

oping conduct disorder.[3] One study of hyperactive boys found that 40 percent had been arrested at least once by age eighteen.[4] The risk of developing a substance use disorder increases when the person with ADHD is hyperactive and increases even more when they have conduct disorder.[5]

While children with ADHD sometimes have learning disabilities, ADHD is not properly categorized as a learning disability in and of itself. The connection is unknown. Dyslexia, for example, is not uncommon among children with ADHD, but it is an entirely different condition and frequently exists without ADHD. Learning disabilities and ADHD do not seem to be genetically connected. Why they sometimes occur in the same individuals is not known. We do know that the primary reason that children with ADHD have learning problems is their inability to pay attention.

Tourette syndrome is a condition associated with unusual and uncontrollable body movements and sometimes involuntary vocal utterances. People with this condition often have ADHD. There is reason to believe, as we will discuss later, that both may result from the same genetic condition.[6] It is possible that Tourette syndrome is a very severe form of ADHD.

While we are not sure just how any of these conditions relate to ADHD, it is important to keep in mind that they often do and that people with ADHD may have a double or triple whammy when living with ADHD is complicated by other conditions as well.

## Self-Defeating Reactions to ADHD

Most people with ADHD—feeling threatened and always at risk—find ways to cope, often before they can put a name to their problems. They develop defensive, and often self-defeating, actions that allow them to "get by."

Lou: *The more I would hide it, the better I would get along. The more I would deny there was anything different about me, the better I could fit in and I really, really wanted to fit in. I did get to a place later in my life where I decided, well, I am different. I'm a free spirit so I don't care about anything or anybody. I'm just going to be a free spirit and be different. And that's it. That wasn't very satisfactory, either.*

Some people cope with ADHD by failing to try, seeking to avoid the pain of failure. They learn to hide their ADHD but in the process hide their own potential.

**Heavy on Self**
by David

Sometimes when the air is angry with noise
all I can do is sit tight,
drawn in, hunched up, taking up little space,
arms close in just trying to hold together
the fragmented moment.
Sometimes as my thoughts collide, jumbled,
speeding with crooked tension,
strung out like fibrous fingers across my stomach,
torrents of fear are released
as I yell at ones I love—sometimes others
(could be dangerous these days).
Sometimes when tasks unravel like thousands of flying fishhooks
endlessly jutting this way and that,
all I can do is avoid their wrath
before they snag me and drag me along.
Sometimes I sit. And sit. And sit
only to think of what I'm not doing that I should be,
that familiar fist in my soul's gut holding my will prisoner,
slamming me down, keeping me back, keeping me heavy on self.

Some people make an art of deliberately underachieving in order to avoid competing and taking the chance of losing. Others take on the role of clown to draw attention away from their failures. Some develop an "I don't care" attitude; others accept the label of "bad," living up to the role ascribed to them already.

David: *Nobody really helped me. Despite all the conferences with teachers, the battles over homework, the wars over a stupid little box the teachers wanted me to look into and connect the lines to correct my nonexistent "vision problem," and numerous trips to psychologists, it was my good old compensating behavior that helped me the most. I learned to get by. To adjust. To take shortcuts. To cheat (not big time but in little ways). To find out what the teacher expected (charm does work). And I survived, even though at times I felt that survival was not what it was cracked up to be. I am quite sure that on more than one occasion I entertained the notion that I would have been a tad bit better off if I had never seen the inside of a school and been raised by wolves instead.*

Some people learn to hide the defects associated with ADHD by avoiding situations in which they might be exposed. They drop out of school early and find jobs in which their defects are less obvious. Settling for less from life allows many ADHD victims to avoid exposing their inadequacies, but they continue to carry the secret shame and dissatisfaction of living below their potential. The really sad part is that so many, in order to survive, learn to live in safe mediocrity.

Dale: *What got me to look at whether I had ADHD was the fact that I was always losing jobs. Over piddling stuff. Over not having my tie tied and that sort of thing. I was not able to be consistent. I've always planned things the night before they were supposed to be done. When the pressure built up so I absolutely had to do something, then I would get it done. It was better "last minute" because the juices would start flowing and the adrenaline pumping and this would motivate me to do the job. Otherwise, it just wouldn't get done. This caused problems because this kind of preparation is not in too many job descriptions. If the task required doing a little bit over a period of time, then forget it. I would tell my boss to "take this job and shove it" before I had another job.*

## Self-Medication

A destructive, though effective, coping strategy used by many people with ADHD is the use of mood-altering substances or behaviors. If the brain chemicals that normally produce feelings of well-being are out of balance, a person will naturally seek ways to right that imbalance. Alcohol is a popular choice for attaining the desired effect.

Other mood-altering substances and behaviors provide a similar payoff. Not only alcohol and other drugs but sometimes eating, excessive sexual activity, spending, or risk taking are used as self-medication to relieve the discomfort associated with ADHD. ADHD people, without being aware of it, are always searching for what they are missing. Mood-altering substances and behaviors seem to supply what they are looking for. Upon making this discovery, the person with ADHD may, for the first time, feel normal. The underlying problem—the genetic defect that causes the neurochemical imbalance—does not go away. But the symptoms are relieved. The jagged edges of overload are smoothed.

### Just Trying to Get Normal

by David

From that first moment, I fell in love
with its love for me.
Good ol' alcohol filled in the holes in my chest
and the cracks in my brain.
It gave me warmth, a security of self,
a self I could know rather than doubt.
It gave me hope,
hope that I could make it in this all-jumbled-up world,
that perhaps the pieces could fit
and I could figure things out,
and maybe—just maybe—I could feel okay.

It could be that the reason it was once believed that the symptoms of ADHD go away in adolescence was because the use of mood-altering substances and behaviors worked so well as self-medication that, when adolescents discovered their effectiveness, observers thought the symptoms had disappeared. The symptoms had actually been "normalized" by the substance or behavior.

Recent studies suggest that the "fly on the wall down the hall is driving me crazy" syndrome does not go away. But when alcohol, drugs, or mood-altering behaviors are used, the symptoms are covered up. The tragedy of this self-medication method of coping is that the ADHD person is genetically at risk of developing a serious addiction. Addiction leads to family problems, school problems, job problems, financial problems, legal problems, and health problems.

The extent of the tragedy is revealed when this person stops using the addictive substance or behavior. The ADHD symptoms come back in full force. In fact, they may come back stronger than ever because of damage done to the neurological system by the drugs or compulsive behavior.

## Effects on the Family

In the past it was believed that poor parenting and dysfunctional family interactions were somehow responsible for the symptoms of ADHD. This creates a stigma for the family that increases feelings of inadequacy and reduces the family's ability to cope and to build a healthy family system.

Attention deficit hyperactivity disorder is not caused by poor parenting. But parenting problems are certainly a result of ADHD in the family. No one is to blame for the genetic defect that causes ADHD. It is the biological symptoms of ADHD that lead to confused parents and dysfunctional families. Understanding this not only improves the way the family views itself but increases its courage to find solutions.

Mary: *I did not find out what was wrong with my son until he was in grade school. I wish I had known when he was a baby that he had attention deficit disorder. I guess I still wouldn't have known what to do, but I don't think I would have felt so frustrated and bewildered. Doug never slept all night until he was two years old. Night after night he would wake up screaming and we couldn't find anything wrong with him. I tried to hold him and soothe him, but he would stiffen and pull away from me. Sometimes this would go on for hours. No doctor was able to help. One doctor prescribed a barbiturate and when it didn't work he increased the dose. But the more we gave him the worse the situation got. I had other children. I was tired all the time and found it difficult to be an adequate parent to any of them. Fortunately Doug was cute and smart and easily entertained in the daytime by the other children. Otherwise I don't think I could have made it. His hyperactivity was a problem in school, though, until he was diagnosed as having ADHD and put on medication.*

Anxiety, anger, and confusion are normal responses of parents and siblings to the behavior of ADHD children. As babies, their crying fatigues and erodes the patience of their parents. Sometimes babies with ADHD are sensitive to touch and consequently do not respond to holding and cuddling as parents expect. The parent may feel rejected by the baby.

> Parents can become just as edgy about being rejected as babies can, and so they may withdraw from their newborns when their overtures are rebuffed.
>
> Lynn Weis, *Attention Deficit Disorder in Adults*

As toddlers and school-age children, their temper tantrums and failure to follow directions may frustrate parents and generate punitive responses. ADHD children demand more attention than the average child, and when parents are unable to meet the demand on their time and energy, they feel inadequate, defeated, and drained. Parenting guidelines for non-ADHD families are of little or no help. Even conscientious and caring parents may be unable to cope. When parents react in anger, they feel guilty and are likely to react to their overreaction with excessive leniency. Inconsistency, the result of harsh punishment followed by leniency, makes the situation worse.

> Carol: *When my kids were trying to get ready for school, things were crazy at our house. I feel so badly now for my poor kids. I didn't know what I could do to help. I had some ideas on how to help at school, but I didn't realize what I could do at home—like softening the environment to provide a soft structure. I never had that myself and I didn't know how to get it. The things that would have really helped my kids they didn't get because the things that would have helped me when I was a child I didn't have.*

Problems *between* parents may erupt because of differing views on how to handle the ADHD child. When nothing seems to change the unwanted behavior, they may blame each other. They may feel, as parents often do, that the child's negative behavior reflects badly on them. So embarrassment and shame intensify the frustration and anxiety, and the cycle continues. Focusing on one child so much changes the dynamics in the family and can damage relationships.

Adding to the problem of having ADHD *or* having a child with it is the high incidence of having ADHD *and* having a child with it. Since

ADHD is genetic in part, both parent and child often have the condition (sometimes both parents or more than one child), complicating family interaction and intensifying the problem. Many children with ADHD have an undiagnosed parent who is also volatile, susceptible to frustration, and overreactive. An ADHD parent with a short fuse is plagued with the same symptoms he or she is attempting to control in the ADHD child. Symptoms clash with symptoms. Parenting is difficult for an ADHD parent even if the child has not inherited the defect; but when both parent and child have the condition, the family may find itself in a state of chaos and confusion—and sometimes abuse.

> Gil: *I am really having a hard time right now. I've got my little son, Donny, with me for a month. It's just Donny and me and we both have ADHD. It's going to be a difficult month, not because I don't want him here but because I'm not able to participate in AA the way that I need to. I don't have anywhere to leave Donny and I don't want to neglect him in any way; he's important to me. We're having a hard time.*

The problem is intensified by society's judgment of parents of ADHD children. How often they hear comments from an "all-knowing" relative or friend describing the appropriate discipline for a hyperactive child: "If that were my child, I know what I would do." The fact of the matter is, most people do not know what they would do in a similar situation. What might work for other children does not necessarily work with an ADHD child. The frustration and confusion of this reality are seeds for conflict and dysfunction within the family.

The problem of ADHD in the family is further complicated if an ADHD parent or teenager in the family is using drugs, alcohol, or mood-altering behaviors to cope with his or her symptoms. This is often the case. The problems of inconsistency and anger that are present in a family dealing with ADHD are increased when addiction is present, and the dysfunction is more severe.

If the addicted person becomes abstinent, the family usually believes that everything will be all right. But they may find that the problems of active addiction are replaced with problems of active ADHD. The family in which there is both ADHD and addiction is so enveloped by shame that healthy interaction is difficult even in caring families. This is their genetic legacy.

## Stigma, Shame, and Self-Fulfilling Prophecy

The ongoing relentless bombardment of augmented stimuli experienced by people with ADHD results in impulsive and defensive reactions. Judged by these behaviors, ADHD people are misunderstood, condemned, and sometimes rejected. Methods used to control or restrict them or force them into more socially acceptable behavior often only further intensify the symptoms and defensive behavior.

David: *Whatever the challenge of any particular school assignment in any particular school year, I was always short on attention, memory, tolerance, and all the other stuff needed to succeed in school. I was particularly short on self-confidence. I was usually "present," but my self-esteem was always "absent." I knew, somewhere in myself, that my problem was that I had a problem; but this knowledge was overshadowed by the painful belief that I was the problem. Me.*

This reaction is very human. When a biologically-based condition generates behavior that is perceived by society as "bad," people with the condition develop a perception of themselves as bad. Shame colors their perceptions of themselves, others, and the world. Most people with ADHD live with the secret conviction that they are dumb or bad or both.

Meryl: *I could not control myself. I'd sit there wiggling and making noises. If someone said, "Sit there and don't move," it was all I could do not to get out of my chair. My mind would wander and the next thing you know I was up out of my chair for something. The person that told me to sit still thought I was just not obeying. It had nothing to do with them. I tried to do what they said, but I actually forgot. Then they would yell at me and I couldn't understand why I was so bad. Why I just couldn't be good.*

The messages that people with ADHD hear over and over again—that they could do better if they would just try harder (when they are doing as well as they know how), that they just don't listen, that they should be like so-and-so, that they cause so much trouble—translate into: *You are bad and you are dumb.* Is it surprising, then, that a person with ADHD is plagued by low self-esteem? Very early in life they develop a deep inner shame, not a shame of what they *do* but shame of what they believe they *are*—defective.

Under such judgments, people with ADHD are often scarred by painful social interactions. Misunderstood and mistreated, they may become scapegoats subjected to psychological and even physical abuse that contributes not only to deep inner shame but eventually to frustration and anger. When the frustration and anger become intolerable and no acceptable ways of coping are found, children with ADHD may become resistant, oppositional, aggressive, and eventually delinquent.

Feeling socially unacceptable, they may seek friendship with other socially unacceptable people, put themselves in socially unacceptable situations, and get drawn into socially unacceptable activities. Then, meeting the criteria for conduct disorder, they are further stigmatized.

## It's Not All Bad

Certainly the problems of ADHD are serious and often devastating, but we don't want to ignore the truth that there are some good things about having ADHD. As a matter of fact, many of the problems connected with it are problems *only because of the reactions of other people* to the symptoms, not because of the symptoms themselves. Many ADHD people are not only intelligent but highly creative. They may not make good grades in school, but they may have spectacular ideas they are unable to communicate to people who are less creative or more conforming. Because they are judged by their behavior, their problems are attributed to a defect in character and the good and beautiful things about them often go unrecognized.

Impulsivity, while not appreciated by those who think through and plan every move, can add zest and fun to life. Creative people are risk takers. They dare to think out of the common mold, to act on their ideas even if those ideas are unexpected and spontaneous.

What is creativity but impulsivity gone right?
        Edward M. Hallowell and John Ratey, *Driven to Distraction*

Because they are dependent on the external to give them structure—because of internal chaos—people with ADHD are sensitive to what is not in place or not right in the environment. They may be able to take preventive action or set things right that others are simply not aware of. Someone has suggested that "scanning" is a better word than "distracted" to describe the ADHD state. The constant scanning of the environment may be a detriment in some places, such as the classroom, but in other circumstances may be quite beneficial, even a survival skill.

> Mike: *Being hypervigilant may not have been so bad for me sometimes. Considering where I lived, it may have kept me from getting stabbed a few times.*

People with ADHD can be sensitive and caring because of their hyperawareness. Their eyes can sweep across a roomful of people and become aware of situations and needs that others simply ignore because they are unaware. This hyperawareness gives the person with ADHD an eye not only for hidden ills around them but hidden beauty.

People with the ability to see and hear so much at one time often have an appreciation of art, music, and nature that simply passes others by. When listening to music they hear and experience every instrument. When looking at a painting they are aware of nuances of color not perceived by those less aware. When walking by the ocean they are aware of the sand beneath their feet, the color of the sky, the sound of the seagull, and the grace of the pelican. They notice the size and shape of the shells, the roar of the sea, the regularity of the waves, the great expanse of the water. And so they have the capacity to experience ecstasy and awe in a way that is unknown to those who can experience only one thing at a time.

> David: *A memorable magic moment occurred for me as I was going through a car wash. A Kenny G CD was on, and as I glided through the suds, I was cleansed by the sounds of the music. Just rub-a-dub-dubbing*

*along through the car wash, that sax and I were one. All around the car, music angels were flitting on shooshing wings delivering their rhythmic embrace, fusing me and settling an always fragile equilibrium with soothing resonance and artful elegance. I felt cleaner than the car, my sparkle enhanced by music's medicine.*

Some people with this special sensitivity feel a special kinship with animals—and animals with them. Perhaps their special sense of awareness creates a special bond.

David: *While visiting the zoo I experienced a special interaction with a baby gorilla. I watched this animal child for a long time playing with his mother. As he played he seemed to be aware of my presence and made eye contact a number of times without stopping his play. He reminded me of a two-year-old child running and jumping, throwing sticks, and turning somersaults. He finally stopped his play and sat down facing me. As our eyes met I gave a slight wave and he responded by reaching out his arms as though he wanted me to pick him up. In that instant all else ceased to exist for me. The world was quiet as that baby and I were the only inhabitants of the earth. I felt a rush of awe, realizing that in this tiny piece of time I was allowed into his world. We had ceased to be of different species. Our spirits touched, transcending boundaries. I had made a sacred connection. I knew I would never be quite the same again.*

People with ADHD often have a special sense of humor. Upside-down pain can be humor on its feet, off and running. Why is an ADHD kid often considered the class clown? Partly because humor is used as a defense against embarrassment, but partly because of a natural wit that pops out before it has a chance to be stifled.

In the expanding community of ADHD people and their supporters, a message of hope and a positive position on the attributes of ADHD are beginning to echo. These attributes include creativity, spontaneity, humor, energy, and determination. Many ADHD people are incredibly successful. In an attempt to promote the positive aspects of the condition, some chapters of Children and Adults with Attention Deficit Disorder (CHADD) circulate lists of illustrious figures who they contend likely suffered from ADHD.

Benjamin Franklin, disorganized and argumentative, flunked out of George Brownell's Academy. He got into trouble as he tried to work in his father's candle shop because his distractible nature led him to explore and to watch the ships come in. But he brimmed with endless ideas and imaginative projects that spilled over into countless businesses such as a newspaper where he wrote, edited, designed, printed, and distributed *Poor Richard's Almanac*. He went on to create one of the first libraries in America. He founded an insurance company, Philadelphia's Public Works Department, and the American Postal Department. And these are just a few of his accomplishments. His inventions include the Franklin Stove, the bifocal lens, a science that tracked storms, and many others. He also signed the Declaration of Independence, wrote the Articles of Confederation, and helped complete the Constitution.

Winston Churchill, before achieving political prominence, was a poor student who couldn't concentrate. His mother once said that Churchill's work was an insult to his intelligence. If he could only have traced out a plan of action for himself and carried it out, she was sure he could be anything he wished but that his thoughtlessness was his worst enemy.

Thomas Alva Edison left school at the age of seven after three months of formal education. He commented in a letter written later in life that he never got along in school. That he was always at the bottom of the class. Edison said, "I used to feel that the teachers did not sympathize with me and that my father thought I was stupid."

Ernest Hemingway complained endlessly that his college courses were boring and that his short attention span convinced him that college was a waste of time. He bounced around the world from adventure to adventure and while doing so became one of America's foremost authors.

Albert Einstein, another poor student, was distracted, socially awkward, messy, and infinitely creative. Other greats who exhibited symptoms of ADHD include Socrates, Isaac Newton, Leonardo da Vinci, Henry Ford, Andrew Carnegie, Napoleon, and John D. Rockefeller.

While these genius-type characters may have had ADHD and successfully overcame this handicap, many do not, especially if the disorder is not diagnosed early. Ordinary schools and "normal" projects tend to work against the creative and intelligent mind. Recognition of ADHD as a neurological disorder can remove the stigma and open the way to appropriate diagnosis and treatment, thus releasing the frustrated potential and hidden abilities of those with ADHD. Likewise, new understanding of the nature of impulsivity and compulsivity and its relation to ADHD can open up new possibilities for winning the battle against addiction. We are beginning to remove the stigma and are well on our way toward a solution.

# 4

## Reward Deficiency: Crime at the Neuron

For thousands of years, people judged self-destructive or anti-social behavior in purely moral terms. People who drank too much alcohol, ate too much rich food, had an ongoing behavior problem (such as what we now call attention deficit hyperactivity disorder), or were in any way compulsive or impulsive, were thought to lack moral fiber, to have no willpower. Or their problems were blamed on "poor upbringing." There are still a lot of questions surrounding such behaviors as to whether they result from a disease, bad behavior, character flaws, poor parenting, or cultural conditioning. Why are some people able to use mood-altering substances in moderation while others are not? Why do some people curtail their appetites for food, sex, or risk taking while others do not? Is "appetite" the same for everyone with differing responses to it or is our behavior a response to varying types and strengths of appetites?

In recent years new light on the subject is showing us how compulsive and impulsive disorders are related to neurochemical deficiencies, excesses, or imbalances. Kenneth Blum has termed this condition the *reward deficiency syndrome*. In order to understand the research connected to RDS we need to understand something of how the brain works.

### How the Brain Communicates

The principal working units of the brain are tiny, complex cells called "neurons." They are the communication centers that send and receive messages about conditions inside and outside the body. Neurons are factories that manufacture the chemical compounds that serve as messengers. They also work as mood-control centers that determine the nature and intensity of our feelings and as action centers that largely control our behavior.

Neurons, each as complex as a computer, communicate by passing packets of messenger molecules from one neuron to the next in the chain. The cell body inside the neuron can be thought of as a tiny chemical factory that manufactures neurotransmitters that carry messages from one neuron to another.

After the neurotransmitters are manufactured in the cell body, they move down tiny tubes to sacks or vesicles located near the end of the neuron. When the neuron is stimulated (by a signal from the nervous system due to something we see, hear, touch, smell, taste, think, feel, or perceive), it releases some of the neurotransmitters. To get to the next neuron the message must cross a gap called the synapse. Neurotransmitters carry the message across the synapse and deliver the message to receptors on the next neuron, which sends the message on in the same way. Each neuron is connected with thousands of others, each sending and receiving messages to and from thousands of others. In this way a single message can quickly reach millions of neurons.

For an insight into just how complex this communication network really is, think about this. There are more than fifty billion neurons in the cortex of the brain—more neurons than there are stars in the universe. The number of possible interneuronal interactions is incomprehensibly large. According to the National Academy of Sciences, a single human brain has a greater number of possible connections among its nerve cells than the total number of atomic particles in the universe.

Some neurons produce neurotransmitters that *excite* the second neuron, while other neurons produce messengers that *inhibit* it. If the messenger from the first neuron tells the second neuron to manufacture a substance that makes you feel good, you begin to feel happy and satisfied. But if the message is to stop the production of the feel-good molecule, you soon feel restless, anxious, irritated, or depressed.

You may experience a craving for a mood-altering substance or feel overwhelmed by the stresses and pressures of normal living.

## Neurotransmitters and Receptors

Neurotransmitters are manufactured in the neuron from amino acids and the supply is controlled by enzymes that have the capacity to destroy neurotransmitters. Normally enzymes keep the supply of neurotransmitters in balance with the demand for normal cell activity. There are two types of neurotransmitters: *monoamines* and *neuropeptides*.

### Monoamines

Monoamines are made of single amino acids derived from food and carried by the blood into the brain. Let's see how they affect us.

*Serotonin:* Its effects are many and varied. Serotonin promotes feelings of well-being and helps us sleep. It reduces feelings that lead to aggression and compulsive behaviors. Serotonin also elevates the pain threshold and helps protect the heart.

*Dopamine:* Dopamine increases feelings of well-being and alertness. It also decreases the desire for compulsive behaviors. An excess of dopamine can lead to irrational behavior or aggression.

*Norepinephrine:* This neurotransmitter is a derivative of dopamine. It energizes, increases feelings of well-being, and may reduce compulsive behavior. Low levels may result in low energy and depression. But an excess of norepinephrine may cause anxiety and increase heart rate and blood pressure.

*GABA:* GABA is a major inhibitor of neurotransmission. It reduces anxiety. It can elevate an individual's pain threshold, heart rate, and blood pressure.

### Neuropeptides

Neuropeptides are neurotransmitters made from linked amino acids called *peptides* that are produced in the brain. There are hundreds of them. We are primarily concerned with the opioid peptides (commonly referred to as opioids) because they are involved with addictive behavior. They are endorphins, enkephalins, and dynorphins.

*Endorphins* reduce pain and anxiety and increase the feeling of well-being. They stimulate the immune system, and they help you learn. They reduce appetite for drug- and alcohol-seeking behavior. Endorphins also affect our reaction to light and darkness.

*Enkephalins,* when present in sufficient supply, reduce pain and anxiety. They are key neurotransmitters in addictive, impulsive, and compulsive behaviors—a shortage increases drug, alcohol, and carbohydrate cravings.

*Dynorphins* play a major role in pain control and help regulate immune response. They stimulate feelings of well-being, regulate sexual appetite, and reduce feelings leading to compulsive behavior. Dynorphins also promote emotional balance and enhance mental activity.

### Neurotransmitter Receptors

Neurotransmitters seek out and attach to receptors on the neuron. The receptors accept only those chemicals whose molecules have a matching shape. In other words, the neurotransmitters fit into receptors in the same way that a key fits a lock. To complicate matters, however, there are three types of receptors for serotonin, five for dopamine, four for norepinephrine, two for GABA (with at least twelve subtypes), and five for opioids, plus a number of subtypes. The receptors will also accept ingested chemicals that mimic the natural brain chemicals. For example, nicotine binds to the acetylcholine receptor. LSD binds to the serotonin receptor. Mescaline binds to the dopamine receptor. Marijuana binds to the THC receptor. Morphine and heroin bind to the opiate receptors.

## The Neurotransmitter Cascade

Neurotransmitters work together in patterns of stimulation or inhibition. The *interaction* of these natural brain messengers has a powerful effect on our emotions and our thinking processes. The interaction usually begins with just one neurotransmitter and then spreads and involves others in a pattern that resembles a cascade. If the result of the cascade action is pleasurable, Kenneth Blum first termed it the "brain reward cascade."

Let's consider one example. The neurotransmitter serotonin tends to help us sleep and reduces anxiety or craving. Serotonin activates receptors that cause the release of enkephalins which inhibits the release of GABA. The inhibition of GABA increases the supply of dopamine, which activates dopamine $D_2$ receptors in an area of the brain called the nucleus acumbens, which we call the reward area of the brain. As this cascade effect progresses, the supply of dopamine increases and we experience a decline in restlessness and anxiety and an increase in feelings of well-being.

The way we think, feel, and behave results from chemical reactions and interactions in our brains. The normal cascade of neurotransmitters provides internal positive reinforcement for the thoughts, feelings, and behaviors that generate it. We tend, then, to repeat actions that cause us to feel less restless and anxious and that allow us to feel complete, satisfied, and competent. We all want to feel good and we seek substances and activities that allow us to experience pleasure and relieve pain.

## Reward Deficiency

But what if something interferes with the normal reward cascade of neurochemicals? This happens if excitatory neurotransmitters are in short supply or blocked at the receptor site, if inhibitory neurotransmitters are oversupplied, or if regulatory enzymes destroy neurotransmitters before they can cross the synapse to reach the receptors. The resulting chemical deficiencies, excesses, or imbalances create discomfort—a *reward deficiency*. The discomfort may take the form of restlessness, anxiety, difficulty focusing, feeling incomplete and inadequate, or hypersensitivity. In turn, these uncomfortable feelings may get expressed as anger, aggressiveness, shyness, hyperactivity, or deviant behavior.

Undesirable changes in the production of neurotransmitters, resulting in an oversupply or shortage, can be caused by many factors:

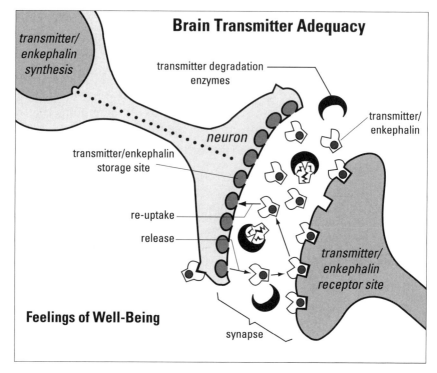

Figure 1 represents *two neurons with normal neurotransmitter activity in the brain.* The first neuron produces adequate amounts of neurotransmitters. Under stimulation these are released into the space between the neurons (known as the synapse). The neurotransmitters then fill the receptor sites in the reward area of the second neuron and a feeling of well-being exists.

ongoing stress or unhappiness, long-term abuse of alcohol or drugs, the effect of toxins inadvertently taken into the body, or structural defects in neurons or in a controlling gene.

Many people are born with an impairment that interferes with the normal reward cascade so they do not get the natural reward from neurochemical interaction that other people get. In 1990, Kenneth Blum, Ernest Noble, and other colleagues identified a defect in the dopamine D2 receptor gene that they found to be associated with al-

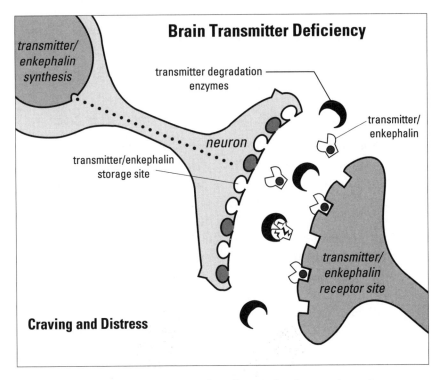

Figure 2 represents *two neurons when the supply of transmitters is inadequate and the receptors are unfilled.* The resulting neuronal activity is experienced as craving and distress.

coholism[1] and that has since been found to be associated with other compulsive and impulsive disorders, including ADHD. This is not an "alcoholism" gene but a gene involving pleasure states in the brain.

The defective gene results in a lack of dopamine receptors, which interferes with the usual neurochemical reward cascade and creates a reward deficiency. The defective gene makes it difficult for neurons to respond to dopamine, the neurotransmitter involved in feelings of pleasure and *regulation of attention.* People with the symptoms of attention deficit hyperactivity disorder are in most cases born with reward deficiency. ADHD is a problem of communication among the neurons. When you disrupt the function in the brain anywhere, you disrupt the ability to pay attention.

> It is the lack of balance, dysregulation of the body's neurological system, that impairs one's ability to pay selective attention to one's surrounding.
>
> David Comings, *Tourette Syndrome and Human Behavior*

Dopamine neurons run through regions of the brain that regulate attention and impulse control. Because dopamine helps us regulate attention, a disruption in the dopamine system results in trouble organizing thoughts, paying attention, and feeling connected. For some time, people treating ADHD wondered why the drug Ritalin, a stimulant, would help hyperactive children become less stimulated. The answer might lie in the cascade theory. Dopamine converts into norepinephrine. ADHD involves an underutilization of dopamine and norepinephrine. Drugs that act on serotonin act on dopamine and norepinephrine. The cascade involving these three neurotransmitters is probably the key to attention deficit hyperactivity disorder.

When there is a short supply of neurotransmitters that inhibit incoming stimuli, too many signals get through and cause overload. This may be the genetic link between attention deficit hyperactivity disorder and compulsive disorders such as substance use disorders and gambling.

## Self-Medicating the Reward Deficiency

Reward deficiency is a predisposing factor for the use of mood-altering substances. People with a reward deficiency may not be able to feel pleasure or relief from pain unless their receptors are stimulated with large amounts of dopamine. How are such large amounts of dopamine released? The surest and most immediate way is by ingesting a mood-altering substance. Ingested drugs allow people with a reward deficiency to control stress and restore a sense of well-being. But why do these substances offer so much relief? Because these substances imitate and fit into the receptors for natural brain chemicals. For example, molecules of opiates (drugs made from the opium

poppy) have the same shape as the naturally produced opioid neurotransmitters. So for people with a reward deficiency, ingested chemicals can do what nature does not. Through use of these mood-altering substances they find what they are missing. When the ingested
mood-altering substances bind to receptor sites intended for natural
chemicals, they create relief, a sense of well-being, and even euphoria.

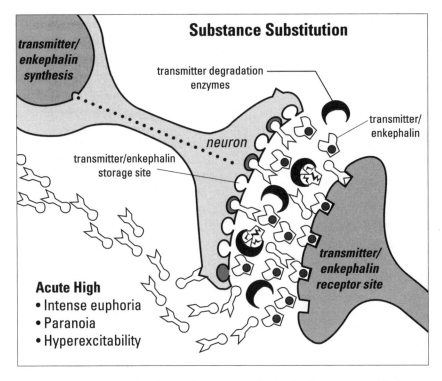

Figure 3 represents *the chemical activity in the brain that occurs with the
"Acute High."* The re-uptake of neurotransmitters is inhibited. This
causes more neurotransmitters to be produced. The addictive substance
also has the ability to attach to reward receptors normally occupied by
neurotransmitters. The overall result is that the synapse is flooded by
both neurotransmitters and addictive substances, causing a feeling of
euphoria.
By Kenneth Blum, Ph.D./Reprinted from *The Addictive Brain* by
NeuroGenesis, Inc.

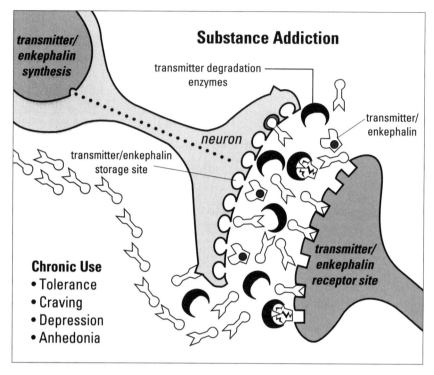

Figure 4 represents *chronic use of an addictive substance*. With continued use, addictive substances further interfere with the release of neuro-transmitters and block the receptor sites in the reward area. At the same time, *the number of receptor sites increases*. It takes more and more of the addictive substance to fill the reward receptors and obtain a "high." Craving remains high as well as a feeling of depression and unhappiness.
By Kenneth Blum, Ph.D./Reprinted from *The Addictive Brain* by NeuroGenesis, Inc.

However, these substances interfere with the brain's natural chem-ical controls. When the brain is flooded with large quantities of such drugs, the nerve cells react by reducing the synthesis and release of neurotransmitters so there are even fewer than before. This explains why, over time, people who use drugs frequently and excessively need more and more of their drug of choice to get the same effect.

When the drug is removed, the brain's natural beneficial chemicals

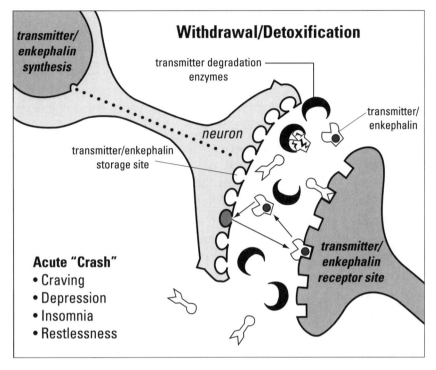

Figure 5 represents *the stage where intervention has taken place.* The addictive agent has been withdrawn. The neuron is producing very little, if any neurotransmitters. Of the few neurotransmitters that are released upon stimulation, only a small percent get to the reward receptor sites. With the increased number of receptor sites, and most of them not being filled, the patient experiences intense craving, insomnia, restlessness, profound depression, total absence of pleasure, and increased feelings of worthlessness.

By Kenneth Blum, Ph.D./Reprinted from *The Addictive Brain* by NeuroGenesis, Inc.

find fewer receptors to which they can bind. This causes nervous excitement or withdrawal, followed by an intense craving for the drug, all of which leads to the continued use of the substance for relief.

People with ADHD use whatever works best for them to relieve their discomfort. Some people do not use drugs but find a behavior that—done excessively—gives them the reward they are seeking.

Mood-altering behaviors also change biochemistry and can be used to medicate a reward deficiency. While substances change mood and perception by binding to receptors intended for natural brain chemicals, behaviors change mood and perception by stimulating the production of the natural brain chemicals. Compulsive behaviors are chosen according to the results they produce. When there is a need for feelings of excitement and stimulation, behaviors are chosen that result in brain chemical interaction that produce those reactions. When there is a need for stress reduction and relaxation, behaviors are chosen that produce those results. Excessive use of a behavior may become compulsive in a continued attempt to self-medicate reward deficiency.

The major compulsive behaviors used to alter mood are gambling and risk taking, working and achieving, exercising, sex and relationships, spending, thrill seeking, and escape (excessive use of movies, television, computer games). These behaviors are used as some people use drugs—to produce euphoria or a rush. For example, gambling produces a high comparable to a cocaine high. With sexual addiction, a sexual encounter may create a high that includes not only the act itself but the whole experience of planning and thinking about it and the activities related to carrying out the plan. Such activities can become as exciting and mood-altering as drug use. A spending spree can create its own intoxication.

> June: *Whenever I anticipated a shopping spree, I felt powerful. I probably should call it a shopping* binge *because that's what it was like. I felt exhilarated by the joy of the hunt, going from one store to another to another, finding what I was looking for, or even what I wasn't looking for. And the activity of buying and buying, even when I was spending way beyond what I could afford, made me excited and actually euphoric.*

Because compulsive behaviors can be used as drugs, people with reward deficiency are at risk of becoming addicted to them with excessive and repeated use. Being born with a genetic defect that affects the neurotransmitter cascade is not the only way for a reward deficiency to develop. For example, it can be created by heavy use of mood-altering substances over a period of time. Or by severe physical or psychological trauma. So if someone does not have the genetic condition, it can be created by environment. It is the combination of nature and nurture together that create the highest risk of addiction. While the genetic condition alone often leads to use of mood-altering substances or behaviors, the risk is increased in certain environmental situations.

> John: *I always felt that everyone else had a secret about life that they weren't letting me in on. My father was an abusive alcoholic and nothing I ever did pleased him. I just couldn't get it right. I couldn't relate to other kids in school. I didn't pass second grade—for not "working up to my potential"—which increased my low self-esteem and my hatred for school. With abuse at home and abuse at school, junior high was total hell except for one thing. That is when I discovered marijuana. When I smoked it I had magic for the first time in my life. It calmed me. It was something I could do and not feel "less than" other people. I had discovered a magic potion.*

People with a reward deficiency are more vulnerable to addiction than other people, not just because they are looking for a way to relieve their discomfort but because something different happens when they use a mood-altering substance or behavior.

# 5

## Addiction: The Pain of the Gain

**R**eward deficiency creates vulnerability to addiction. When a substance or behavior works to relieve pain or increase pleasure the chance of continued use is high. The probability that people with a reward deficiency will self-medicate regularly and heavily is very great. It is not only because of this that they are at risk of addiction. Metabolic studies have shown us that when people with a predisposition for alcoholism drink, they have a different physiological response than someone without the predisposition, a reaction to alcohol that increases their risk of addiction if they continue to drink.

While using a mood-altering substance works to relieve the symptoms of reward deficiency and is a pleasant experience, addiction is not. Addiction is painful, life-threatening, and not a solution. It is important to understand that social use of a mood-altering substance or behavior is entirely different from addiction. We can alter the way we feel with mood-altering substances or mood-altering behaviors without being addicted. Addiction is characterized by compulsion and loss of control.

When someone who has found a mood-altering solution to reward deficiency continues to use—knowing that the source of relief is causing problems and is even life-threatening—this is addiction. Addiction is distinguished from social use by the lack of freedom of choice. Using a mood-altering substance or behavior is a choice; addiction is not. All addiction begins with use, but all use does not lead to addiction.

Addiction is a physical disease. It is properly classified with cancer, heart disease, and diabetes as a chronic illness that produces long-term physical, psychological, and social damage. While addiction—at least alcoholism and some drug addictions—is currently accepted by many as a disease, until recently it was considered a moral issue. Even among those who have accepted addiction as a disease, there is still a common belief that its underlying cause is psychological. Current research, however, challenges the notion that addiction is primarily psychological and is giving us more and more evidence that the body of a person who becomes addicted does not react to mood-altering substances or behaviors in the same way as the body of a person who does not become addicted.

## Addiction Is a Physical Disease

The first major insight into the true nature of addiction came through early research into the causes of alcoholism. A book called *The Disease Concept of Alcoholism,* written in 1960 by Dr. E.M. Jellinek, provided new insights. It defined alcoholism as *a chronic disease that was sometimes inborn, characterized by a biochemical sensitivity to alcohol, and often accompanied by psychological strain and feelings of inadequacy.* Dr. Jellinek concluded that people drink because it helps them turn away from their emotional pain.

While he had no real scientific proof of his theory, Jellinek's book stimulated research into the nature and causes of addiction. Let's look at what research is showing us about addiction and the brain. It is difficult to experiment on living human brains. But scientists have been able to examine the brains of alcoholic mice to search for causes of addiction. Some early research showed that laboratory mice and rats responded to alcohol much the same as humans. Some become addicted. And they experience withdrawal symptoms when alcohol is denied. It was also found that certain genetic strains of mice have an inborn preference for alcohol over water. These mice are born alcoholics!

The research that followed slowly removed alcoholism and other compulsive behaviors from the realm of speculation and subjected them to rigorous scientific analysis. One of the first discoveries was that when mice drink alcohol, their brains convert part of the alcohol into an opiatelike substance that resembles morphine. In other words, the brain makes its own drugs!

This chemical that forms when alcohol is ingested has been given the tongue-twisting name of *tetrahydroisoquinoline*—thankfully shortened to TIQ (or THIQ). Scientists found that when alcohol is ingested, TIQ molecules are formed and provide *temporary* feelings of well-being. This was an exciting finding. It provided the first scientific clue that addiction might have a biochemical origin. But why did TIQ in the brain create feelings of well-being and euphoria?

As early as the 1950s scientists suspected that addictive substances must bind in some way to specific sites in neurons of the brain, locking onto receptors specifically shaped to receive them, but it wasn't until the early 1970s that opiate receptors were found in mammalian brains. If so, there must be receptor sites in the brain specifically for receiving opiates (drugs that contain opium), to which TIQ attaches when it is converted from alcohol.

Scientists learned that the brain can recognize subtle differences in the chemical makeup of a variety of drugs in the opiate family. Opiates usually exist in two forms. These two forms are chemically identical but are mirror images of each other. Remarkably, the brain distinguishes between these two forms and responds to only one of them. This indicates a highly selective process of matching opiate molecules with specific receptors.

But where were these sites located? The first clues came in the '60s and '70s from researchers working in different parts of the world making similar discoveries. They found evidence supporting the idea that opiates bind to receptors specifically shaped to receive the opiate molecules and that the location of the opiate receptor sites corresponds to locations in the brain where opiates are known to be active.[1] Since most people live their lives without ever taking opiates, the finding of neuron receptors for opiates raised a puzzling question: *Why does nature create receptors designed to receive a drug derived from poppies?*

A reasonable explanation was that *the brain manufactures compounds similar to the opiates* that relieve pain or generate feelings of well-being or euphoria. If so, it would be natural for the brain to have receptors that accept all such compounds.

These speculations opened the door to one of the most exciting competitions in the history of science. Independent teams raced to isolate and identify the brain's natural opiates.[2] In 1975 a morphine-like material was isolated in pig brain.[3] This compound was found not only in areas associated with pain but also in areas associated with well-being or pleasure. The compound was called *enkephalins* from the Greek word meaning "in the head."[4] Since that time numerous other natural opioids have been identified.

It was found that feelings of well-being are triggered when the opiate receptor sites in the brain are filled with natural opioids. But when the natural opioids are in short supply, the person feels restless and discontented and experiences some form of compulsive craving, which brings us back to TIQ and explains how it is involved in addiction.

When alcohol is metabolized in the body it is first changed into acetaldehyde. Studies have shown that when alcoholics ingest alcohol they have higher levels of acetaldehyde in their blood than nonalcoholics.[5] Other studies have shown that this is also often true for sons of alcoholics before they have any history of drinking.[6] Acetaldehyde converts to TIQ in the brain; higher levels of acetaldehyde result in greater amounts of TIQ.

When acetaldehyde converts to TIQ, the TIQ floods the brain's opiate receptors and creates feelings of well-being and euphoria. But the effect is relatively short-lived; craving soon begins again. When the receptor sites are filled with TIQ, the natural opioids can't enter and provide long-term satisfaction. Because the effects of TIQ wear off quickly, the tendency is to drink more and more alcohol to feel good again. Alcohol provides temporary relief, but this relief comes with a high price tag. If more alcohol is ingested, more TIQ forms and fills the vacant sites, blocking off the natural opioids as well as other neurotransmitters like dopamine. This only creates more TIQ and the result is a self-destructive spiral.

Literally hundreds of experiments have come together to suggest that craving involves abnormalities in the reward cascade in the reward site area of the brain. While these abnormalities result in substance use disorders, there is a high probability that other abnormal behaviors such as pathological gambling, compulsive sex, and impulsiveness share the same biogenetic syndrome. If this view is correct, we can then derive a simple conclusion: Genetic anomalies disrupt the normal functioning of the reward cascade. The defects in the reward cascade work in three destructive modes: They interfere with the normal release of dopamine; they distort the structure and function of the dopamine receptors; and they cause a reduction in the number of dopamine receptor sites.

It is believed that when victims of reward deficiency self-medicate, the alcohol, cocaine, heroin, glucose, or certain behaviors offset the deficiency by inducing the release of abnormal amounts of dopamine. While the mechanisms by which these diverse agents work may differ, the net result is similar—temporary relief.[7]

Since most scientists agree that addictive behaviors are polygenetic (more than one gene is involved in determining predisposition), we can speculate on future findings. This speculation postulates that in addition to the defective pleasure gene (which we believe to be the gene that controls the dopamine D2 receptor that normally regulates pleasurable responses), there may be other defective genes that determine *specific* pleasure-seeking activity. While the abnormal D2 receptor gene creates a general need, other genes dictate the craving for a particular abusable substance. One gene may interfere with the synthesis of enkephalin or serotonin, leading to a craving for alcohol. Another gene may interfere with the synthesis of a natural stimulant such as alpha endorphin, leading to a craving for cocaine. Still another gene may interfere with the synthesis of natural brain morphine, leading to a craving for morphine or heroin. And another gene may interfere with the function of the glucose receptor, leading to a craving for sugar or carbohydrate bingeing.

Some people are born more susceptible to becoming addicted than other people. People with a genetic predisposition are not predestined to develop addiction, but they are of high risk because of reward deficiency and because of the way their bodies respond to mood-altering substances or behaviors. *Different people have different levels of genetic or inherited susceptibility for addiction and the strength of the predisposition will influence how much use over what period of time will be necessary for addiction to develop.* People with ADHD are of very high risk because the use of mood-altering substances or behaviors brings so much relief and pleasure that continued and long-term use as self-medication is very likely.

## The Progression of Addiction

The use of mood-altering substances or mood-altering behaviors almost always begins as a pleasant experience (especially for people who have the brain chemistry abnormalities or imbalances present in those with ADHD). But over time, continued use of the substance or behavior by someone who is predisposed for addiction leads to a cycle that creates problems and pain that only more use of the substance or behavior can alleviate. The symptoms of addiction develop gradually over time in a pattern that looks very much like what happened to Carol as she progressed through these stages of addiction.

### Immediate Gratification

As noted in the previous chapter, for people experiencing the pain of ADHD, use of a mood-altering substance or behavior provides an immediate payoff: pleasure or pain relief. You must remember that people who are predisposed to becoming addicted, as people with ADHD are, do not have the same reaction to mood-altering substances or behaviors as people without this predisposition.

Almost everyone has a positive experience from using a mood-altering substance or behavior. That is why so many people drink socially. The drug or behavior produces pleasure and reduces physical and emotional pain. But for the person with ADHD, the payoff is more intense and more dramatic. This powerful short-term gain creates the illusion that the mood-altering substance or behavior is beneficial and will make life not only more pleasurable but more productive. The person feels more in control, more capable of thinking clearly, and more comfortable emotionally.

> Carol: *Throughout my childhood I was looking for relief from the symptoms of my ADHD (although then I didn't know that was what was wrong with me). When I was a freshman in high school, I went to visit a friend who lived on a farm. I loved the farm. We rode horses and walked out in the fields, and I was in heaven. One weekend my friend's dad was shearing the sheep. We'd round them up for him. We were actually getting to help with the work all day long. We came in hot and sweaty and my friend's mom had supper ready for us. The family drank wine with their meals. They served homemade wine in these aluminum tumblers, all different colors. When the tumblers were cold, they got real frosty looking. So I had a tumbler of wine. I drank my wine and it tasted so good. And I ate a little bit. Her dad asked, "Do you want some more?" I remember him chuckling a little. I had another glass. I'd had little sneaks before but never was there wine on the table where I could just drink it.*
>
> *We went to a rodeo and a rodeo dance that night. I don't remember much about the dance except meeting a guy who was a freshman in college and a football player. I danced with him all night and every bit of my awkwardness disappeared. All I can remember is feeling good and dancing with that guy and thinking I was pretty cool. And I directly associate those feelings with the wine.*
>
> *That was the beginning of my regular use. It was like a screen or filter. It felt really good in the beginning. It was like magic. Sometimes I still miss that feeling.*
>
> *I can also remember how much I loved to go out to a dance and drink where there was a band. I would get totally involved in the sound. You could feel it vibrate on the floor and everything else would be incidental. Who I was dancing with was incidental. I could get totally involved in the music and not worry about anything.*

The positive experiences of early-stage addiction interfere with the ability to recognize that addiction is developing because the condition at this point appears to be a benefit and allows the person to enjoy the euphoria of the mood-altering substance or behavior without paying any price.

### The Pain of the Gain

## Painful Consequences

The immediate gratification from the use of a mood-altering substance or behavior is eventually followed by pain. This pain is the direct consequence of using the addictive drug or behavior. It may develop within hours of use or it may be delayed. The long-term painful consequences may take days, weeks, or years to develop. The consequences usually affect all areas of life: Problems arise at school or on the job; medical problems develop; problems with the law such as driving under the influence or buying or selling an illegal substance may occur; problems with parents, spouse, children, or friends arise and grow worse.

Carol: *When I drank I felt more sophisticated, more popular. As a teenager my ADHD caused me to feel insecure and fearful. When I went out with somebody I liked I would get loaded so I wouldn't feel so awkward. But I would end up doing something stupid and never hear from the guy again.*

*By this time I would stop at a bar on my way home from school. I was drinking and using speed instead of doing my homework. My grades suffered. I surrounded myself with people who were willing to drink like I wanted to drink. This caused me to be ostracized by some people who had been my friends during the early part of high school. I tricked myself into thinking that was all right because I was a free spirit. I could do whatever I wanted and didn't have to pay attention to the norms of society because I was an exception. That way I didn't have to feel the pain of what was already happening as a result of drinking—making bad choices.*

*Drinking caused me to skip school two weeks straight when I was a senior. I got drunk one night and was afraid to go home, so I spent the night away. Things just escalated to the point that I was afraid to go home or to school. During that two-week period of time I met a guy. He gave me an engagement ring while we were driving down the street. There were other people in the car and I thought, "What a hoot. This guy is a free spirit like me." I took the ring and I married him. I stayed married for three days, but I got pregnant. So I couldn't go to college. I really made a mess of everything. I wanted and loved my son, but I was not ready to be the mother he deserved.*

## Using to Relieve the Pain of Using

People with ADHD who are addicted have learned that their drug or behavior of choice *works* to relieve pain. So the more pain the addiction causes them, the more they will use to relieve that pain. More pain, more use; more use, more pain. While relieving the discomfort of attention deficit, the addiction is causing new pain. The need to use for pain relief blocks the awareness that the drug or behavior is causing consequences that, in the long run, will become more devastating than the pain of ADHD.

Other people think they are being irresponsible. But at this point the people who are addicted cannot choose to drink or use responsibly. Not aware that the only alternative to continued problems and progression of the disease of addiction is abstinence, they continue to make irresponsible choices while attempting to drink or use the same as other people they know.

> Carol: *I always felt guilty and embarrassed about drinking or how I behaved while I was drinking or not knowing what I had done. I was afraid of what I would find out. So to cope with those feelings I drank more. I was no longer drinking just to cope with the symptoms of ADHD but also to cope with the consequences of my addiction. In many ways the solution to my problems was the cause of my problems. I would say I didn't care, I was a free spirit, I didn't give a hoot. But I did. After I had children I felt guilty about staying out late and not getting up in time to get my kids off to school properly. I would send them off less than spick-and-span and then feel really bad about it. Then I would drink more because I felt so bad about not being a good mother, about not taking care of things. I would deny even to myself why I was doing it. It doesn't make sense to do more of what is causing the problem, but that's what I did.*

## Tolerance/Dependence

During the early stage of addiction, tolerance increases. This means that someone who is becoming addicted can use larger and larger quantities before getting the desired effect or experiencing the same consequences. More and more of the drug or behavior is needed to produce the same effect. The body adapts to higher levels of the substance or behavior and accepts that level as normal. Without the substance or behavior, the person does not feel normal.

While tolerance is increasing, however, so is dependence. Though there may be no conscious awareness of it, there is a growing *need* to use as well as a growing desire. Cells of the body—especially in the brain and liver—are changing in order to tolerate larger and larger quantities of the chemical or behavior. The brain is becoming reliant on the mood-altering substance and starts shutting down its own production of chemicals. Larger quantities are required to get the same effect. The more of the mood-altering substance or behavior used to generate good feelings, the less one learns to use more effective ways to cope with feelings, situations, and people.

People with ADHD who use mood-altering substances do not learn other ways of coping and living with their symptoms because they can rely on their mood-altering substance or behavior. Eventually, tolerance begins to decrease while dependence increases. When this happens, the person is no longer able to use the same quantities without becoming intoxicated or creating problems.

Carol: *I remember the first time I realized I needed to drink. Because of all my assorted problems, my son and I were living in a small trailer with a friend and her two kids. I was drinking a lot to relieve the pain of not being able to succeed and not being able to provide for my son. I always managed to have a waitress job or some kind of job through all my drinking. One day I was out looking for a better job. I had worked the night before and it was ten or eleven in the morning. My friend was with me and I needed a drink. It was the first time I knew I needed a drink. We went into a bar and I had a Bloody Mary followed by something else. I felt better after a few drinks. I knew at that moment in time, I had a problem. I knew. I didn't know it was called dependence, but I knew my body needed alcohol. I had to have a drink. And I got physical relief from it. That day, that hour, I knew I was in trouble. But that knowledge didn't stay with me. I was able to put it out of conscious awareness—by evening!*

**Attempts to Control**

Becoming aware that using is creating pain, the addicted person may attempt to control use. Then *not using* begins to create pain. This is *withdrawal*. Most of the pain of withdrawal is created by the body's need for the addictive substance. But part of it is due to the emotional reaction of giving up such an important and comforting part of one's life. Acute physical withdrawal stops within a few days, but for the person with ADHD, the problems may just be beginning. The symptoms of ADHD reemerge when the addicted person is no longer using the mood-altering substance or behavior to take them away. So the addict finds another way to relieve the symptoms of ADHD, which often means switching to another addictive substance or behavior.

> Carol: *When I finally decided drinking wasn't that much fun anymore, I switched to pot. It was never really the drug for me, but it did cause me problems. Too many people were coming over for too many hours to smoke pot and it was interrupting my life. So I decided I wasn't going to smoke it for a while. Instead I drank wine. Then I switched from wine to beer. I kept switching from one thing to another. And that went on for years. I drank coffee with bennies in it. I did a lot of things like promise myself I would only drink on weekends. I was kind of like that person in* Learning to Live Again *who promised herself she wouldn't drink before lunch and then one day one of her children asked her why they had to eat lunch at 9:30. I did have short periods of time when I was totally abstinent, but then my ADHD symptoms got worse and worse and I told myself I just needed a little something to get me through.*

**Slipping Back (To Relieve the Pain of Not Using)**

As the ADHD symptoms intensify and interfere more and more with the ability to function, the compulsion to use becomes stronger and stronger. The pain, obsession, and compulsion become so strong that feelings and emotions become distorted. Finally the urge to use becomes so great that the person cannot resist it and then *uses to relieve the pain of not using.* At first the person may use in moderation or may control the frequency of use. But addiction renders its victims unable to use in moderation and they soon begin slipping further and further back.

> Carol: *I finally decided to quit entirely to prove I didn't have a problem, that I didn't have to drink. I went for almost a year, but it was so uncomfortable that I can't remember much else about it. After I went so long I figured I had proved I could, so I started having a little. I tried to set limits. I would make resolutions not to drink when I had to get home and fix dinner for the kids. And I could do it for a while, maybe a week. Then I would get so uncomfortable I would break my resolution. I'd say, "I will just go in with the girls after work and have one wine spritzer and then I'll leave." But the rest of them would go home and I would be there until the bar closed.*

**Loss of Control**

Once using begins again, the cycle starts all over. The addicted person is incapable of functioning normally without the addictive drug or compulsive behavior. The chronic stage of addiction is marked by deterioration of body, mind, and spirit. All body systems can be affected at this stage as addiction-related illnesses develop. Guilt and shame increase as a person begins violating his or her own value system (lying about frequency and quantity, neglecting family, ignoring responsibilities). In spite of vows and promises and strong intentions, life is consumed by the need to use.

> Carol: *There came a time when my drinking was totally out of control. I was out on the edge, drinking, partying. I left my kids with their father and just gave up all pretenses of normalcy.*

# Delusion

The long-term pain and dysfunction trigger delusional thinking. In the beginning, addicted people are unaware of their addiction because the good experiences (especially relief from ADHD symptoms) outweigh the bad. As the addiction progresses they are not aware that the problems they are having are related to use of mood-altering substance or behavior. Eventually, because the effects of addiction impair thinking and judgment, they are removed from the reality of the addiction.

There are a number of circumstances that work together to keep the addicted person from becoming aware that use of a mood-altering substance or behavior is not normal and is causing problems. These circumstances keep the addict in a state of delusion.

*Neurological Impairments:* Alcohol and other drugs can damage the structure of the brain or alter brain chemistry levels, creating neurological impairments that distort reality.

*Blackouts:* These are periods of time when a person is drinking that he or she is unable to remember. They are blank spots in memory. Because of no memory of what happened during the blackouts, the person can go on as though the events did not happen, and truly, in his or her mind, they didn't.

*Intoxication:* When people are intoxicated, their perception of reality is distorted. Incidents that to other people may seem shameful, embarrassing, or irresponsible, in the perception of the intoxicated person may seem perfectly normal, even delightful or noble. If intoxication is a regular part of someone's life, then the perception of life is distorted.

*The Need to Survive and Feel Pleasure*: Addiction forces those affected by it to adopt some delusional thinking in order to survive. Because their feelings are painful and at times uncontrollable, they come to believe that it is only with addictive use that their feelings become manageable. They perceive the world as a painful, unsafe place to be, and addictive use makes life seem more manageable.

Life is tough for people with ADHD and they may believe that their drug or behavior of choice is their only source of pleasure. They may actually feel that in order to continue to survive in this painful world they *must* have their addiction. *What they believe will happen to them if they stop using may seem more terrifying than death.*

## Recovery

Even though at this point the picture looks pretty bleak, *addiction is not a hopeless condition.* Like other chronic conditions, it is treatable. It is not curable, but it can be controlled. *Total abstinence is necessary for recovery.* Any use will keep addiction active. Abstinence alone, however, is not recovery. In most cases, a choice to stop is not sufficient unless there is treatment of some type—especially when there is ADHD. Many people make an honest commitment to stop, but without help from outside of themselves they cannot keep that commitment.

*It is also very important to understand that once addiction has developed in the person with ADHD, treating ADHD alone is not enough.* No effective or lasting healing can take place until addictive substances are removed from the body and treatment for addiction takes place.

The first step of treatment is removing the toxic substance from the body—detoxification. Acute withdrawal symptoms that emerge with abstinence can be very serious. Withdrawal is a medical problem and should be treated by a physician. A common method of detox is administering a substitute drug and gradually decreasing the dose until the withdrawal symptoms have subsided. The substitute drug must be entirely removed from the body before the person is considered fully detoxed and drug-free. The major goal here is to replace neurotransmitter levels and bring them back as close to normal as possible as soon as possible. A nutritional supplement of amino acids from which brain chemicals are manufactured can be very helpful in accomplishing this. We will talk more about this in a later chapter.

The value of counseling for a person beginning recovery from addiction is facilitating the development of skills to manage the condition and to prevent relapse. A counselor who understands the strength of addiction and the necessity of a change in lifestyle can be a great aid to recovery. It is also helpful to be in a therapy group with other people who are learning how to be sober and who help each other see things more clearly.

For long-term comfortable sobriety, a twelve-step support group is important. Many recovering people honestly feel that they owe their lives to Alcoholics Anonymous or Narcotics Anonymous. AA is free, it is readily available, and the only requirement for membership is an honest desire to stop drinking.

A plan for taking care of self is an essential part of recovery. This plan needs to include regular activities that support recovery: good nutrition, exercise, fun, relaxation, activities for spiritual growth and personal development. When an addicted person chooses abstinence, he or she has come to realize that the pain of drinking or drug use is even more severe than the pain it relieves. Giving up addictive use is not an easy step.

The most difficult thing about abstinence is pretty much everything. Change takes place, and it takes place all at once. People who have struggled with addiction and ADHD must let go of the only hope they have found to help them feel good, to help them survive. They have to let go because the pain of using has become more severe than the pain of not using. Now they have only the promise of others that they will, at some point, be able to feel good again. It feels as though they must let go of the branch that has so tentatively held them from falling into the chasm. They must let go and they don't yet have the knowledge and experience to make a parachute. Treatment and self-care that address both addiction and ADHD are that parachute, offering support as the necessary changes are made. Eventually the changes that *are* recovery become the reason for recovery. And that which was feared becomes that which gives life meaning.

# 6

## It's Baaack!

**There are painful symptoms of addiction that occur when some-** one is using—symptoms that motivate the addicted person to give up addictive use. When the pain becomes severe enough, addicted people usually choose recovery. Recovery requires abstinence, but abstinence triggers *new* symptoms.

Some abstinence-based symptoms occur within hours after using stops (acute withdrawal). These symptoms last only a few days (though they can be very serious). And then there are other symptoms that emerge after acute withdrawal has passed.

Joel: *I felt very excited about being sober. I was on a natural high. Finally, I had done this thing that I'd wanted to do for so long and I felt wonderful. I received lots of positive reinforcement from the people around me. My family was both proud and excited about the new changes they saw in me. And at AA meetings, people rallied around me. I was feeling very good about my life and the positive steps I was taking. But at the same time, other feelings were starting to creep in. I experienced some anxiety. My stress tolerance was much lower than it had been. And I found myself becoming easily aggravated and irritated. My short-term memory was letting me down. I was also more easily distracted by extraneous stimuli. In many ways, despite the fact that I was feeling very good about my life and my new direction, I also found myself wondering what in the world was wrong. I had quit drinking so everything should be all right now. But when I got real honest with myself I knew it wasn't.*

It is very often a surprise to recovering people, when they get through the pain of acute withdrawal and have a short period of feeling better, that rather than experiencing decreasing pain, their discomfort increases. Some of these painful symptoms result from alterations in brain chemistry due to drug use. For people who have been self-medicating their ADHD, however, some of these symptoms are the return of ADHD symptoms. The return of ADHD symptoms can complicate sobriety and easily lead to relapse when the person experiencing them doesn't understand what is happening and doesn't know what to do about the symptoms.

## Abstinence-Based Symptoms

Stimulus augmentation (overload) not only returns but is more severe than before addictive use. This happens because brain chemistry is altered by mood-altering substances and behaviors. The number of receptor sites has decreased, the reward cascade is further distorted, and the reward deficiency is more severe than before addictive use began.

One possibility is that lowered $D_2$ receptors due to the addiction tend to exacerbate stress. Because recovering people are stress-sensitive, they are likely to overreact to anything that generates any level of anxiety at all. This overreaction creates problems that increase stress levels.

### Tangles

by David

Coat hangers, paper clips, bits and pieces of tattered papers,
fishhooks, the miscellaneous drawer with pins and junk,
all appropriate for this funk I've fallen in
this new day of darkness.
What is it anyway with all these tangly, clangy,
never-to-be-put-together things that seem to appreciate your wrath?

Those hangers like grafts of fused angles,
never to be separated or used, but inviting outbursts
where throwing them quickly cannot be quick enough.
And paper clips! I can never justify the time it takes to untangle them.
They don't warrant any time at all.

Fishhooks, all crooked together, present one pointed dilemma,
for there is never time to untangle them.
Certainly not while fishing

does one want to fiddle with these mingled points and barbs.
And when the great fishing expedition is over,
one just wants to forget the whole tangled mess.

With even more severe stimulus augmentation, it becomes harder to concentrate. A person who is easily distracted and unable to concentrate will have memory problems. Stress levels increase as the recovering person overreacts to environmental stimuli and also to the inability to concentrate and to remember. Forgetting important aspects of daily living creates new problems and adds to the stress. And anxiety in turn intensifies the severity of stimulus augmentation, creating an escalating cycle.

> Nicky: *It's very difficult with so much change going on. In early sobriety, change is all that happens. So with my ADHD I feel overwhelmed a good part of the time. I have always had great difficulty juggling my responsibilities, especially when I was working full-time. Where I worked, things were very inconsistent. There were changes all the time. Every day that I went to work, I didn't know what to expect. As I would drive to work, feelings of anxiety would set in. I felt I was walking into a whirlwind when I got there. My memory would go. I could not keep my train of thought or set my priorities and schedule for the day. I could not adapt. In order to function effectively, I needed to know what my responsibilities and duties were. This gives me the ability to focus. I constantly felt anxious and fearful. This caused me to be reactive in my approach to my responsibilities. And I don't feel effective when I am in a reactive mode.*

An abstinence-based symptom that is often misunderstood is accident proneness. Most people are confused to discover that physical coordination is impaired by abstinence, as it seems logical that coordination would be improved by removing the mood-altering substance from the body and the brain. But this is not so surprising when you remember that some people with attention deficit hyperactivity disorder have coordination problems. So when the substance that has been "normalizing" the brain is removed, it is natural that coordination problems return.

Some symptoms experienced by abstinent addicts complicate recovery for the person with ADHD, even though they are not related to ADHD. One of these is state-dependent learning. which also affects memory. We remember things best when we are in the same mental state as when we learned them. So if someone learns to study, talk with the opposite sex, or bowl while high or intoxicated, that person will have some difficulty remembering how to do these things when not in the same drug-induced state.

> Sue: *I avoided dancing when I got sober because the first few times I tried to dance I felt awkward and ill at ease. I felt like I had four feet and I just couldn't dance anymore. So whenever my husband wanted to go dancing, I would find ways to avoid it. My husband loves to dance and wanted me to overcome my feelings of awkwardness. So he suggested that we practice in the privacy of our home. We did this for a time and it was easy for me to regain the skill of dancing. It wasn't long before I again became comfortable going dancing with my husband.*

For the ADHD person who begins alcohol or other drug use during adolescence or before, many of the skills related to maturing and socialization are learned while under the influence of a mood-altering substance and will be affected in sobriety. It is important to know that skills learned while under the influence are easily relearned in sobriety with a little practice. But a person who isn't aware of this could easily overreact to this inability to perform certain tasks that were done comfortably while using.

The difficulty concentrating, remembering, tolerating noise, and managing stress in recovery causes some people to feel they may be going crazy. They are not. It is the return of their ADHD symptoms intensified by the changes in the brain brought about by the use of mood-altering substances. The anxiety that accompanies the symptoms of ADHD and the increased anxiety due to the changes of recovery, *plus* the anxiety of not understanding what is happening, increase the risk of relapse.

> Carol: *Two weeks after I got sober and was just beginning to be aware of what I now know were the return of ADHD symptoms, I was taking a real estate class. The class met at night. It was bitter cold. When I came out after class, even though I was sober, I couldn't find my car. It was*

*very confusing because I knew I was sober and I still couldn't find my car. It felt scary. When I was drinking there was a reason for getting lost or not being able to find things. Now I didn't have an excuse. Now I was sober and I couldn't find my car. I thought I had left it in a certain parking lot. I walked around several blocks, and it was bitter cold.*

*I felt really stupid and finally went back to the building. It was the Knights of Columbus building. The upstairs was locked so I went downstairs and sat in the bar. I must have looked a fright because the bartender said, "My God, what's wrong? Can I get you a drink?" I said no and I'm still thankful that I was able to say no. I told him I couldn't find my car.*

*I had to call my mother and I know she thought, "What on earth?" But my folks came and got me. They could see I wasn't drunk. Mom was so disgusted. At least that's how I interpreted it. But I think they were disappointed. They really wanted me to get my act together.*

Recovery from the damage of addiction requires abstinence. But— catch-22—the damage, along with the return of ADHD, interferes with the ability to abstain. Most people are aware, at least on a subconscious level, that alcohol or other drugs will relieve their pain and allow them to feel normal for a little while. Unfortunately, relief is short-lived as the pain of addictive living returns. It is of vital importance, then, to get treatment for *both* ADHD and addiction in order to manage both conditions for a comfortable sobriety and healthy life.

Brian: *I have ADD and was also addicted to alcohol. For years, I used other drugs as well. I would try anything to make myself feel better. I finally realized that my life was a complete mess and that sobriety was the only answer. So I got sober and stayed that way for a little while. Then I relapsed. This happened over and over again and the effects were devastating. But I kept trying because I wanted sobriety so badly. Finally, I realized that my life was at stake. If I kept up this lifestyle, I knew I would die. I had to do something to interrupt this pattern of relapsing. My most serious abstinence-based symptom was stimulus augmentation. And I realized that I had to have peace and quiet to survive. So I bought a small piece of land outside of town where I could escape the city noise. I kept my job in town, but every evening I knew that I had a place to go where I could find quiet and peace. In this way I was able to interrupt the pattern of relapsing. I have now maintained ten years of continuous sobriety.*

## Substitute Addictions

Recovering addicts who have ADHD are at high risk of developing a substitute addiction to deal with their pain. In the past, they have used their addiction for pain relief. It is the only way they know to feel better. When they give up their drug of choice, they quite naturally look for other sources of relief.

These substitutes can become new addictions or reactivate the original addiction. Many people relapse to their primary drug as a result of trying controlled use of other mood-altering drugs. Alcoholics may substitute marijuana; people who have used illegal drugs may use alcohol. Cocaine addicts are at much higher risk of returning to cocaine use if they drink socially than if they abstain from all mood-altering drugs, including alcohol. Cocaine may also be used as a substitute for the heroin rush. Recovering alcoholics who use marijuana are at high risk of returning to alcohol use.

A large number of people recovering from addiction increase their use of nicotine, caffeine, and sugar when they begin abstinence from their drug of choice—often unaware that these are mood-altering chemicals. These substitutes induce good feelings by releasing dopamine into the reward areas of brain.

Sarah: *I didn't have much trouble with withdrawal when I stopped drinking, and I never craved alcohol. But I had a constant craving for something. I started drinking an extra cup of coffee in the morning (to get going) and found myself going to the vending machine for a Coke as soon as I arrived at work (to get started). I got one of those giant mugs and brought it to work. I kept it beside me and refilled it throughout the day (to keep me going). I relaxed with several cups of coffee after dinner (to wind down). When anyone suggested that I might be drinking too much caffeine or that it might be related to my restlessness and hyperactivity I would say, "It is the only vice I have left, and it's better than drinking."*

It is true that consuming large amounts of caffeine was less destructive for Sarah than drinking alcohol, but her addiction to caffeine caused other problems (such as the inability to sleep). Sarah had found a substitute addiction. Like many recovering people, she took the fastest and easiest route to alter her brain chemistry. There are healthy and unhealthy ways to do that. Healthy ways include improving nutrition, exercising, and finding new ways to have fun.

Yes, some addictions are more harmful than others. And some chemical addictions, such as alcohol, cocaine, or heroin, are more dangerous than addiction to caffeine, nicotine, or chocolate. In most cases caffeine addiction will not cause the same type of severe judgment and behavior problems that result from alcohol or marijuana addiction. But these substances, especially nicotine, are harmful to the body even when there are no other problems. The American Cancer Society reports that more people die from cancer caused by nicotine addiction than by abuse of any other drug (and for some people it is very difficult to stop smoking because of the highly addictive nature of nicotine).

Some people do not use another chemical addiction to feel better but instead develop a problem with gambling, obsessive sexual activity, excessive spending, overworking, overeating, excessive exercise, thrill seeking, or escape through television and movies in order to medicate the reward deficiency. These things are not in and of themselves harmful. They can be used in a healthy way or, if used obsessively and compulsively, in an unhealthy way. Regarding these activities, the important thing is not so much *what* is done as *how* it is done. Total abstinence from these behaviors is not usually possible or even desirable. So it is necessary to change the way they are done so they no longer create problems.

> Clay: *If I get overwhelmed personally, it is easy for me to move right into being a workaholic and just stay at work. And, of course, then my work doesn't really suffer too much at first because I get a lot done. I get really organized and I am being productive, productive, productive. Well, you can only do that until you burn out. And then you are not efficient at work and those personal problems catch up with you anyway.*

Changing from one addiction to another is not full recovery. Full recovery means learning to live addiction-free while using healthy ways to manage the symptoms of ADHD. It means *acceptance* of both ADHD and addiction and the need for changes in lifestyle. It means learning as much as possible about both conditions and finding ways to feel good other than addictive ways.

> Jason: *After I gave up drinking, I needed something to fill the vacancy left in my life. So I started smoking. I also ordered more Cokes and other caffeinated drinks. And because sweets seemed more tempting than ever, I ate more rich desserts. It didn't take long before this increased intake of sweets made me feel very sluggish. And the extra caffeine was causing me to feel much more stressed than usual. I finally realized that the changes I was making in my behavior were not good changes. Smoking is a serious health hazard and was an unwise substitute. And the changes I'd made in my eating habits were not positive either.*
>
> *I began to look for a healthy habit and finally decided to learn to play golf. I took lessons and became a pretty good golfer. I got some positive feedback from learning how to play golf well, and the exercise made me feel great. I put aside nicotine, sugar, and caffeine entirely. I have benefited a great deal from learning to play golf. I felt satisfaction in learning a new sport, my health has improved from the exercise, and I have experienced a sense of well-being. Learning to play golf was a good choice for me.*

## Shame

The shame connected with ADHD and addiction complicates recovery from both. In addition, the recovering person is dealing with the shame and embarrassment of abstinence-based symptoms and, quite often, the shame of relapse. People with ADHD carry an undeserved burden of shame from childhood. They develop a deep-seated perception of themselves as defective. We talked in chapter two about the repeated messages that children with ADHD receive from others that confirm the belief that they are defective: *You just don't try. Sit still. Pay attention. Concentrate. You are interrupting.* These messages translate into: (1) You are *dumb* or (2) You are *bad*. If you hear the same messages over and over, you come to believe they are true whether or not they are. To make a piñata you can blow up a balloon and put papier-mâché around it. When the papier-mâché dries and you let the air out of the balloon, the piñata retains the shape of the balloon. In the same way, our perception of ourselves takes on the shape of the messages we receive and keeps that shape when we are no longer aware of the source.

The unanswered whys cause ADHD people to question their own worth. *Why can't I pay attention? Why do I have to be constantly bouncing from idea to idea and from project to project, never to finish anything? Why don't I listen or follow directions? Why do I do things I have promised myself I won't do?*

### The Shame of Addiction

Despite findings that substantiate the fact that addiction is a physiological disorder, there are still many people who think it is due to a character defect, lack of willpower, or undisciplined living. In addition, addictive behavior is usually harmful to others. Addicted people do things while using that they would not do while sober. They usually hurt the people they love most. They may do things that are illegal or in violation of their own value systems. These "shameful" behaviors intensify the shame that comes from having ADHD so that the person eventually sees himself or herself as worthless. *I am bad. I am weak-willed. I am hopeless. I can't do anything worthwhile. I am unworthy of good things.*

### The Shame of Abstinence-Based Symptoms

The inability to remember, to solve usually simple problems, or to stay in control of emotions leads to diminished self-esteem. A person having these reactions to sobriety feels incompetent, embarrassed, and not okay. Diminished self-esteem and fear of failure interfere with productive living.

The inability to attain a comfortable sobriety raises some more whys. *Why do I get angry at the most trivial things? Why am I so mad at God and myself so often? Why can't I enjoy the sobriety I have worked so hard to attain? Why can't I get it right?*

Without being consciously aware of it, people experiencing abstinence-based symptoms learn to live defensively, always attempting to keep others from seeing their inadequacies. Their periodic confusion, anger, hypervigilance, memory problems, and elevated stress levels are hidden as much as possible. If people find out—that they are dumb, defective, or bad—they will be shamed even more.

### The Shame of Relapse

People who relapse think it is their fault; and other people think so too. They are considered unmotivated and lacking in willpower. But the truth is that people who relapse are not always unmotivated to recover. And people who are willing to try over and over again to get sober and stay sober show a great deal of willpower.

The messages people who have relapsed hear most often are that they didn't try hard enough and don't want sobriety badly enough. For people who can't stay sober because of the intensity of abstinence-based symptoms, these messages increase stress and shame.

Relapse piles shame on top of shame. *Why is it that I just cannot do what I know I should do? Why is it that I just cannot stay sober? Why is it that I cannot amount to anything? Why am I so weak?* Relapse again reinforces the shame messages. *I am weak-willed, constitutionally incapable, not trying hard enough.* Self-disgust seems more justified when relapse verifies that the labels and messages are true. *I really am bad and dumb.*

When we have the perception that we are shameful, we live in fear of being found out. This is the "I am" shame. *I am dumb* (but no one can ever know). *I am bad* (but I must keep people from finding out). *I am defective* (but I would rather die than let it be exposed). *I must hide what I am. I have to keep from being discovered. I cannot risk the shame of exposure. If the world knows it I will die.*

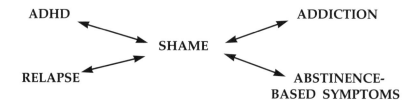

Shame puts recovering people at risk of relapse. Shame keeps them living in such a way that they can continue to hide the shameful "truth." They use avoidance behaviors to keep what they believe about themselves a secret, sometimes even from themselves. They may appear to function very well because their behavior prevents discovery. The great waste in using avoidance behaviors to prevent exposure is in the time, energy, and talent consumed. Strengths, talents, and gifts used for survival are *not* being used for creative and productive living.

> Lyle: *As a child I didn't know I had attention deficit hyperactivity disorder. But I developed the belief that I was dumb from messages I got in school. "Lyle is not doing as well as he could." "Lyle could do so much better if he would try." I was trying, so the obvious conclusion was that I was not capable of doing as well as my teachers expected. I must be dumb. Being dumb was so shameful for me that I went to great lengths to keep it hidden. I went through college and became quite successful. But still I lived in fear that people would find out the truth about me. I read extensively to create the illusion of being "intellectual." I became conversant in topics that don't require right or wrong answers (religion, philosophy) in order to avoid subjects that required me to analyze and come up with correct answers (science and math). My life became so stressful from the continual effort to prevent exposure that out of exhaustion I finally acknowledged, "Yes, there is something wrong with me. I do have trouble learning. I have trouble concentrating and I have trouble thinking clearly sometimes. Maybe this does not mean I am dumb, but I need to find out what it does mean." It took all the courage I could muster to risk being tested (the tests could prove that what I feared most was true). I found out that I had ADHD, but I also found out that I have a very high IQ. Now I have to keep reminding myself, "I'm not dumb. I'm smart."*

## Regression

In the absence of a program of self-care to manage the reemerging symptoms of ADHD and overcome the shame associated with them, a gradual regression away from the commitment to recovery begins to develop, usually out of conscious awareness. The combination of painful symptoms, stress, and shame can create an anxiety crisis that triggers this regression that spirals out of control.

## Anxiety Crisis

Because of the relationship between stress and physical symptoms, recovering people are vulnerable during times of high anxiety and are at risk of responding to the anxiety in a self-defeating way. The anxiety situation can be physiological (pain, sickness, fatigue, improper nutrition) or situational (change of job, family circumstances, living conditions). It can be real or imagined. It can come from strong feelings of anger, fear, or depression. It can even come from happy events that create change. A certain amount of stress usually accompanies change.

Situations most likely to trigger an anxiety crisis are those where avoidance behaviors may not work to protect one's shameful "truth" from being discovered. This anxiety arises from the terror that the "real self" will be revealed. Most people with ADHD have spent their lives developing avoidance behaviors to protect them from what they believe to be true about themselves. When confronted with a situation where these behaviors may not work to hide the shameful secret that they are "dumb" or "bad," high levels of anxiety, usually suppressed, will occur.

Anxiety is not necessarily bad. It is not the situation but the reaction to it that determines whether regression is triggered or the anxiety is used as an opportunity. The word "crisis" is defined by Webster's as the *turning point for better or worse*. A crisis is the turning point when a recovering person either faces anxiety and progresses in recovery or retreats into avoidance behaviors that allow regression to progress.

## Self-Defeating Self-Talk

When we experience anxiety, we talk to ourselves. If what we say to ourselves helps us face anxiety and use it as an opportunity, this is positive self-talk. If what we say increases the anxiety so that we continue regressing, it is self-defeating. Actually, we talk to ourselves in our minds all the time, but in the midst of anxiety we are at high risk of this self-talk being self-defeating.

Self-talk is a normal, healthy process of conversing with ourselves using words, pictures, and sensations. It is what we say to ourselves, statements and messages we give ourselves, sometimes whole conversations we have with ourselves. It is normal and helps us solve problems, make plans, and think things through. By talking things over with ourselves we are better able to reconcile what is going on outside with what is happening inside.

Self-defeating self-talk, though, reduces problem-solving ability and renders a person less able to take constructive action. Instead of clarifying options, it restricts them. It traps a person into circular thinking or thought regurgitation where thoughts run through the mind over and over again, creating negative emotions and images. Instead of encouraging us to face reality and move forward, it encourages us to escape and do things that make matters worse instead of better. The ability to interrupt the self-defeating self-talk cycle is harder for the ADHD person because of impaired neurological functioning and because of years of shame-based thinking.

Self-defeating self-talk messages of a recovering ADHD person usually are some form of the shameful beliefs *I am bad* or *I am dumb.* The words may be different, but the underlying message is there. *I can never do anything right. I'm hopeless. I'm a failure. I can never succeed. I'm unworthy.*

## Self-Defeating Behavior

When we believe something is true, we act as though it is true. When acted out, self-talk messages become self-fulfilling prophecies that document their "truth." The reactions we get from others when we act them out further confirm them. Someone who says to herself, "No one will like me," acts as if no one will like her, so probably will not get close enough to others for them to like her. This confirms what she really believes, which is that she is unlovable.

Someone who says to himself, "I can never succeed," probably will not try. There is no surer way to fail than not trying. One of the saddest things about having ADHD is all the possibilities that never materialize because fear of failure results in failure to try.

Jeffrey: *I always thought I was dumb. While I had a lot of reinforcement to believe this from teachers and from my peers, intelligence tests indicated otherwise. But because I so firmly believed I was dumb, I developed test anxiety. Anytime that I was given a test of any kind, I panicked. All the information I knew seemed to evaporate as soon as I heard the word "test."*

*In spite of the belief I held about myself, I wanted very much to go to college. I had a dream: to become a high school football coach. But when I learned I would have to take an entrance exam to be admitted to college, I was devastated. And of course there would be tests in all my classes. The fear of taking tests was so paralyzing that I gave up my dream. I decided not to go to college because I was certain that I couldn't pass any of the required tests.*

Living out a self-defeating message reinforces its reality. It then escapes out of the mind into the here-and-now for everyone to see. It becomes a concrete manifestation of what the person believes. The negative emotions that fueled the self-talk now energize behavior. There is a cumulative effect as the regression spirals. Shame becomes stronger, anxiety intensifies, self-talk speeds up and becomes more self-defeating, behavior is reinforced.

**Sense of Powerlessness**

When people act out self-talk and get feedback that confirms their self-defeating messages, they come to believe these messages so firmly that they feel powerless to change. Acting as if the messages are true causes others to act as if they are true; and the person comes to believe *the messages will always be true.* This creates feelings of helplessness and hopelessness. The person feels powerless to change anything and has an overwhelming sense of hopelessness.

**Against the World**

by David

Most every time I turn around I bump hard into myself,
trying to get out of my way;
darting this direction and that, waging self-war;
eyes vigilant, scanning for dark inequity;
latching onto other's frowns thinking they may know my ways;
hoping to justify internal discord.

Nothing fits; all tilted masses of juts and jangles
that won't slide into sequence or habitual order and function.
Even the air is colliding upon itself
with molecules no doubt confused of their purpose or plan.

The person feels trapped and defeated and may be immobilized by feelings of loss and deprivation. The only way he knows to relieve this torture is to use a mood-altering substance or behavior, which will create a different set of problems. The only solution is no solution.

The feeling of deprivation reminds him of what he has lost: his faithful friend, the drug or compulsive behavior. He will never have it again. He has not only lost the mood-altering substance or behavior but the life that went along with it. He feels overwhelmed by the losses, the despair, and the hopelessness without a way to relieve the pain. What was supposed to make things better (sobriety) hasn't.

When we believe there isn't anything we can do to change things, we are not likely to try to do anything to change them. And so we stay locked in powerlessness. When we believe something is possible we put more energy into doing it than if we really don't believe it can happen. So hopelessness keeps us locked in powerlessness. *Hope is the catalyst for empowerment.* To make life different, we have to believe we have the power to make it different.

## Conflicts

If a person does not do something to interrupt the downward spiral by finding some other options, at this point she will spiral rapidly into conflict—conflict with self and with others. When an addicted person feels trapped in deprivation, there is war going on between the only two options she can see: (1) being deprived of the pleasure and relief of the addictive substance or behavior or (2) using it again and losing all the gains of sobriety. Neither option is something to look forward to for the rest of her life. Feeling defeated and trapped produces anger and frustration and a need to find someone or something to blame. It is normal to feel angry when feeling so powerless. Life is not fair and that is reason to be angry. The internal anger causes external conflicts. Conflicts begin to escalate to the point that others react, creating new cycles of frustration and anger.

### Risky Choices

In order to relieve the pain of deprivation, hopelessness, and conflict, people in regression begin to make some risky choices. Life has become so uncomfortable that pain casts a shadow over everything and they begin using poor judgment, taking chances that jeopardize sobriety. They stop doing what they know is healthful for them.

When life is out of harmony, daily structure begins to break down. Good self-care is no longer a priority. Exercise, good nutrition, twelve-step meetings go by the wayside.

At this point people in regression are looking for pain relief and they may choose solutions that put ongoing recovery at risk. They may begin using a substitute addiction—gambling, sex, food, spending—to reduce stress.

They may brush up against their primary addiction without actually using—going to a bar to "listen to the band," keeping booze in the house "in case someone comes by," associating with old drugging buddies because "no on else understands." Eventually this leads to "having just one" and perhaps a short period of controlled use. People at this stage of regression are making their way back to what they know will relieve their pain, unrestricted addictive use.

## Loss of Control

Once controlled use begins, it is a short distance to out-of-control use. At first this self-medication works to improve functioning and relieve pain. Before long, however, life is again out of control and relapsers are paying the price with harmful consequences of their choices. And with the return of the pain, there is also a return of shame and hopelessness.

It takes great courage at this point to reach out for help. But ADHD people are usually people of courage because of what they have faced in life and the necessity to overcome hardship and to keep trying. Because of this courage, recovering ADHD people are often willing to try again and again to attain ongoing sobriety. We know remarkable stories of the lengths to which they have been willing to go to make it. With new information and resources that have not always been available, there is new reason for hope. Hope that recovery can be not only less painful but actually joyful and fulfilling.

Gerrie: *Shortly after I learned that stimulus augmentation was part of my ADHD, I was invited to speak at a meeting of Narcotics Anonymous. The room was set up to accommodate a dinner beforehand, the meeting, then a dance after the meeting. The podium was in the center of the front of the room. This was a family affair, so there were children running around the area where my podium was.*

*There was so much going on during the meeting that I was unable to keep a single train of thought. The children were making noise. People were coughing. There was a lot of commotion. When the children crossed by me as I was speaking, I would lose my train of thought and have to start on a different subject. When I finished my talk, I felt as if I had done a terrible job. Shame and guilt began to spiral. However, I did remember what I had learned about stimulus augmentation, and I realized I was responding like this because of the way my brain works. I tried not to focus on the shame, but instead on the opportunity of sharing my story, especially my attention problems. By changing my focus, I was able to avoid spiraling down into the shame.*

*It was really hard for me, however, to be up in front of all those people. I felt very high stress levels and when I would just pause to grasp a word, I would lose my train of thought. I wanted the audience to think I was capable of doing this.*

*The moment those people left and I was alone, I felt myself sinking in shame. And the negative self-talk came flooding in with the shame. And that's when I came home and called David and he helped me reperceive the situation by sharing that he had experienced those situations many times and lived through them and that they would get easier. I was then able to get back up and speak again. By accepting my own limitations, I was able to do a pretty good job.*

# 7

## Reward Deficiency Syndrome: Genetic Blueprints for Behavioral Disorders

The number of people who suffer from addictive, compulsive, and impulsive disorders is staggering. In the United States alone, there are eighteen million people with alcoholism, twenty-eight million children of alcoholics, six million people addicted to cocaine, 14.9 million who abuse other substances, twenty-five million addicted to nicotine, fifty-four million who are obese (20 percent overweight), 3.39 million school-age children with attention deficit hyperactivity disorder, 625,000 with Tourette syndrome; and 448,000 who have the problem of compulsive gambling. The most recent studies indicate that a common genetic factor may link these addictive, compulsive, and behavioral disorders.[1]

### It's in the Genes
by David
He mourns, stews, frets, and wails.
He cries and tries and still he fails.
He's worn, weary, frayed at the seams.
Must be, he figures, those ol' *blue* genes.

Folklore has provided anecdotal evidence that substance-use disorders, compulsive activity, and a *wide range* of behavioral disorders have a genetic link. Science is now finding supporting evidence for this connection. Although at first glance this may be disheartening to people with ADHD and their families, the linkage is actually encouraging. Until recently the causes of ADHD and other related behavioral disorders have been locked in mystery. But the conclusion of recent research seems inescapable: Defective genes, causing abnormalities in brain chemistry, are responsible for a whole range of compulsive diseases and abnormal behaviors. *Thus, what we have learned about the genetics and brain chemistry of compulsive disorders has a direct application to ADHD.*

## Reward Deficiency Genes

As we have already mentioned, the earliest scientific confirmation of the role of genes in the causes of alcoholism came from studies of laboratory animals and gave clear indication that alcoholism is genetic—it can be passed from one generation to the next through the genes.

The first proof that this theory applied to humans came when, through numerous studies, it was found that biological children of alcoholics are more than three times as likely to become alcoholic as the children of nonalcoholics.[2] A different sort of confirmation came in the late 1970s when brain waves of boys who were the sons of alcoholic fathers were compared with those of boys whose fathers were nonalcoholic.[3] None of the subjects, age seven to thirteen, had ever used alcohol or drugs. Researchers found that the brain wave called P300 (or P3) was much smaller in the sons of alcoholic fathers than comparable waves in the sons of nonalcoholic fathers. The importance of this information is that it gives strong evidence that children of alcoholics have unique characteristics that are genetically, not environmentally, determined.

With the accumulation of evidence pointing overwhelmingly to the genetic factor in predisposition to alcoholism, scientists began to look for a gene or a set of genes that could be identified as the causative factor. The problem was dishearteningly complex. Each individual has one hundred thousand genes and a billion pairs of DNA stored in twenty-three chromosomes. In a system this complex, how could a researcher hope to find a gene or a group of genes responsible for an effect such as alcoholism?

When Drs. Kenneth Blum and Ernest Noble[4] decided to tackle the problem they had one simplifying factor working in their favor. Studies of the reward area in the brain had shown that neurotransmitters such as serotonin, dopamine, GABA, and opioids are almost certainly involved in generating feelings of well-being or craving. And craving is a key factor in addiction.

Dr. Blum concluded, then, that any gene that influenced the production or metabolism of these chemical messengers or affected their receptors on adjacent neurons, might be the culprit. If this proved correct, it narrowed the field of candidate genes, reducing the magnitude of the problem from one hundred thousand possibilities to less than one hundred—still formidable, but approachable.

Dr. Noble had a large collection of frozen brains of individuals who had died of severe alcoholism and a group of brains from nonalcoholics that could be used for comparison. The history of each alcoholic brain was known in clinical detail. Tissues from these brains would provide ideal sources of DNA for studying both genes and receptors, making it possible to investigate not only suspect genes but any associated impairment of receptor function as well.

For a more complete description of our search for a gene associated with alcoholism, see appendix A. We were eventually able to make the connection with the dopamine D2 receptor gene. The results were dramatic. There are two variants of the dopamine D2 gene, called the "A1 allele," and the "A2 allele." After testing DNA from the total sample, including both alcoholics and nonalcoholics, we found that 69 percent of the alcoholics *had* the A1 allele and 31 percent did not. Of the nonalcoholics 80 percent did *not* have the A1 allele, while 20 percent did.

Their discovery indicated a strong association between this variant of the gene and the severe form of alcoholism we were dealing with in our experiment. The finding does not prove that the A1 allele of the dopamine D2 receptor gene is the *single* cause of this type of alcoholism, but it is a powerful indication that it is involved or associated with it. Let us not forget that 31 percent of the alcoholics did *not* have the A1 allele. This suggests not only that there may be more than one gene associated with alcoholism but also more than one type of alcoholism.

Furthermore, the fact that 20 percent of the nonalcoholics had the

A1 allele suggests the possibility that this variant gene may result in conditions other than alcoholism. In other words, it is likely that this is a *reward deficiency* gene rather than an alcoholism gene. People with this gene may not develop alcoholism but they may develop some other compulsive disorder. This is not like the gene for brown eyes that always results in brown eyes. The presence of the A1 allele of the dopamine D2 receptor gene is a *predisposing* gene—if you have it you are at high risk of developing alcoholism or some other compulsive or impulsive disorder.

Since this initial finding, a small number of laboratories have questioned the Blum and Noble finding, but a review of the laboratory work of those who have not been able to support the finding shows that *these samples were not limited to severe forms of alcoholism*, as was their study. Fourteen independent laboratories here and abroad, however, *have* supported the finding that the D2 gene variant is a causative factor in severe forms of alcoholism—though probably not in milder forms.

It is important to note, also, that since the original study, *the presence of the A1 allele of the dopamine D2 receptor gene has been found in children not yet exposed to alcohol, indicating that it is not a result of alcoholism but a cause.* The lack of dopamine receptors in individuals who are deficient in the A1 allele may have an important bearing on their inability to cope with *stress.* Dopamine is known to reduce stress, and if there is a shortage of dopamine receptors, stress reduction does not happen. As stress rises, therefore, the individual may turn to substances or activities that release additional quantities of dopamine in an attempt to gain temporary relief. Alcohol, cocaine, marijuana, nicotine, and carbohydrates are all substances that can cause such a release of dopamine in the brain, thereby bringing about a temporary relief. They can be used singly, in combination, or interchangeably.

For the person suffering from ADHD, this is a finding of crucial importance. The underlying concept is that the dopamine system (and other dopamine genes), in particular the D2 receptor gene, is deeply involved in rewarding us with good feelings. Indeed, a number of scientists have suggested that the D2 gene be called the "reward gene" because it produces a reward of good feelings.

We have previously mentioned that a particular abnormality of a brain wave called P300 has been linked not only to active alcoholics but to their sons who have never drunk alcohol. Additional studies show that this abnormal P300 wave in children of alcoholics predicted future substance-use disorders. In children carrying this abnormal P300 wave, significant numbers drank more alcohol, smoked more cigarettes, and used more marijuana.

Recently, Dr. Kenneth Blum and Dr. Eric Braverman[5] and also Dr. Ernest Noble and associates[6] found a significant correlation between abnormal P300 wave activity and the A1 allele of the dopamine D2 receptor gene. This finding suggests that there is a link between this abnormal brain wave and the dopaminergic system. Since the P300 wave abnormality has been shown to be related to heredity, this link increases the possibility that the dopamine D2 receptor gene connection to substance use disorders is related to genetic factors.

## Reward Deficiency Syndrome

This work has sparked numerous studies of similar associations of gene variants with a wide spectrum of related compulsive disorders, including ADHD. At long last we are beginning to understand how and why genetics plays such a major role in behavioral problems. A deficiency of dopamine D2 receptor genes predisposes certain individuals to a reward deficiency. This gives rise to a wide range of impulsive, addictive, compulsive disorders: ADHD, Tourette syndrome, alcoholism, drug dependence, compulsive overeating, pathological gambling, excessive sexual activity, conduct disorder, and post-traumatic stress disorder (PTSD.) One study has shown that 59 percent of Vietnam veterans with post-traumatic stress disorder carried the D2 gene variant, compared with only 5 percent of those who did not (remember that the A1 allele of the dopamine D2 receptor gene is related to the inability to manage stress.)[7]

While other genes playing a role in these interrelated disorders are still to be identified, the concept of the reward deficiency syndrome (RDS) unites addictive, impulsive, and compulsive behaviors and may explain, for the first time, the way in which simple genetic conditions give rise to complex aberrant behavior. A deficiency of the reward or "feel good" chemicals in the brain creates discomfort and cravings that lead to behaviors that provide the good feelings that are missing. Let's look at some of the conditions, in addition to alcoholism, that result from this deficiency and are reward deficiency syndrome disorders.

### Drug Dependence

In the past quarter century, there has been a dramatic escalation in the use of illicit drugs in the United States. The drug that has attracted the most serious attention in recent years is cocaine. This chemical can bring intense pleasure to the user, but unfortunately these effects are temporary, and the aftermath can be addiction and severe mental and physiological harm.

Various psychological or social theories have been advanced to account for the abuse of cocaine and other illicit drugs. In contrast to alcoholism, however, where growing empirical evidence is implicating hereditary factors, relatively little is known about the genetics of human cocaine dependence. There is growing evidence, though, that hereditary factors *are* involved in the use and abuse of cocaine and other illicit drugs.

Although little is known about the genetics of cocaine dependence, extensive scientific data are available on the effects of cocaine on brain chemistry. The current favored view is that the system that utilizes dopamine in the brain plays an important, if not a key role, in the pleasurable effects of cocaine.

About 52 percent of cocaine addicts have the A1 allele of the dopamine D2 receptor gene.[8] Of addicts whose background includes the following, the prevalence of the A1 allele is as high as 87 percent: early childhood deviant behavior, use of higher potency cocaine ("crack" cocaine is a high-potency form), and parental substance use disorder.[9]

A survey by the National Institute of Drug Abuse revealed that in five independent studies, the A1 allele was significantly associated with polysubstance dependence.[10] Another study found that the presence of the A1 allele was associated with an increase in the amount of money spent for drugs by polysubstance-dependent subjects.[11]

Cocaine addiction is found to be present in higher than average rates in individuals with histories of attention deficit disorder, and treated cocaine addicts showed better treatment outcomes if they concurrently received treatment for the attention deficit.[12]

## Smoking

Twenty-five percent of the adult population of the United States are smokers. Tobacco smoking represents a serious health hazard and is associated with a number of major diseases, such as lung cancer and cardiovascular problems. In 1990, smoking-related illnesses accounted for nearly one in five deaths. Smoking is considered by most health professionals to be the single most important source of preventable premature death in the United States.

The question of environmental versus genetic causes of diseases associated with tobacco abuse has been a subject of great controversy. Smokers find it very difficult to stop smoking, and most experience withdrawal symptoms typical of other addictions.

> Becky: *Quitting smoking was very difficult for me. Cigarettes seemed to help me concentrate and focus. I really missed not smoking when the kids were home after school and I was preparing dinner. Noise levels were higher, and I was usually drinking coffee and smoking while I had three or four pots on the stove. Not only did I draw that cigarette in but I also had something in my hand, something to focus on. This produced a centeredness that helped to relieve my stress in addition to the nicotine that made me feel better.*

While environmental factors may play an important role in cigarette use, studies suggest that the acquisition of the smoking habit and its persistence are strongly influenced by hereditary factors. Of particular significance are studies of identical twins that show that when one twin smokes, the other tends to smoke.[13] In one study, twins were surveyed twice, sixteen years apart. This allowed an examination of genetic factors in all aspects of smoking—initiation, maintenance, and quitting. In general, whatever happened to one identical twin happened to the other. This included nonsmoking, smoking, and quitting smoking. These similarities did not appear in the nonidentical twins. This suggests a strong genetic component in smoking behavior.[14]

One study found that the higher the prevalence of the A1 allele, the earlier the age of onset of smoking, the greater the amount of smoking, and the greater the difficulty experienced in attempting to stop smoking.[15] A study of the A1 allele in smokers and ex-smokers showed that the prevalence of the A1 allele was highest in current smokers, lower in those who had stopped smoking, and lowest in those who had never smoked.[16]

### Compulsive Gambling

Pathological gambling has many similarities to substance use disorders. Clinicians have noticed in gamblers an aroused euphoric state comparable to the "high" derived from cocaine and other drugs, the presence of a distinct craving for the "feel" of gambling, the development of tolerance (a need to take greater risk and make larger bets in order to reach a desired level of excitement), and symptoms similar to withdrawal (anxiety or irritability when no "action" is available).[17]

While pathological gambling is a more socially acceptable addiction than substance addictions, the negative effects can be devastating on the individual and the family. Dr. David Comings and associates have sought to determine if an A1 allele relationship is present in pathological gambling. They found that in a sample of pathological gamblers, 50.9 percent carried the A1 allele, and the more severe the gambling problem, the higher the percentage of A1 allele.[18] Furthermore, if the individual had drug problems—along with gambling problems—and was a male, the percentage rose to 70 percent.

### Tourette Syndrome

Over one hundred years ago French neurologist Giles de la Tourette first described a condition characterized by compulsive swearing, multiple muscle tics, and loud vocal noises. This disorder usually appeared in children between seven and ten years of age, and males were more often affected than females. Tourette suggested that this condition might be inherited because it seemed to "run in families." This view was strengthened by later research.[19] Summaries of large numbers of patients with Tourette syndrome showed that one-third had a family history of the disease.[20]

Observing that stress worsens Tourette symptoms, David Comings suggested in his book *Tourette Syndrome and Human Behavior* that genetic anomalies in the reward system of the brain—particularly in the dopamine system—may be responsible for predisposition to the onset of the disease. Comings and his colleagues reported that 44.9 percent of individuals diagnosed with Tourette syndrome carried the A1 allele. The prevalence of the A1 allele increased with the severity of the cases.

Comings has now concluded: "Tourette syndrome is a complex, neuropsychiatric spectrum disorder that includes ADHD . . . Tourette syndrome is a severe form of ADHD and may have the same genetic origin."[21]

### Attention Deficit Hyperactivity Disorder

A study of ADHD children by David Comings found that *the A1 allele of the dopamine D2 receptor gene was present in 49 percent of the ADHD children compared to only 27 percent of the controls*.[22] Moreover, he and his group have found ADHD to be associated with abnormalities in *two other* important dopaminergic genes.[23] The major finding of the Comings group is that while the dopamine D2 receptor gene has the strongest association with ADHD, the other two genes may act as modifiers to the dopamine D2 receptor gene. What is more important is that when the severity of ADHD was measured using a standard test, it was found that individuals that possessed all three of the abnormal gene forms scored highest in severity when compared to individuals that had one, two, or none of these genetic anomalies.

A number of laboratories have been actively searching for a gene in a family of genes associated with ADHD. In this regard, a gene associated with the thyroid hormone has been associated with ADHD.[24]

What is quite interesting is that the thyroid complex may influence the dopaminergic system thought to be involved in ADHD.

Our original findings regarding the dopamine D2 receptor gene and addictive behaviors and Comings's recent findings associating genes related to the dopaminergic system[25] point seriously to a significant genetic cause of ADHD. Given the frequent association of ADHD with substance use disorders and a wide range of behavior disorders, it seems reasonable to suggest that *childhood ADHD may be a predisposing factor in all of these disorders.* Establishing the link between ADHD and other genetic disorders should provide insight that will influence treatment.

Not everyone agrees on the relationship between ADHD in childhood and the risk of addiction later in life. In order to be fair to those who do not agree that there is a relationship—which is the basic premise of this book—we offer the view of a leading researcher in the substance disorder field, Dr. Marc Schuckit of the University of California School of Medicine in San Diego. He has reviewed a number of studies and points out that:

> If a question regarding the tie between the symptoms of hyperactivity in childhood and adult alcohol or drug dependence is taken literally, there is clearly a relationship. Unfortunately, most of the published investigations did not go the important step further and evaluate whether the association with substance-use disorders applies to true ADHD in the absence of evidence of conduct disorder.[26]

This suggests that when the symptoms of ADHD are accompanied by symptoms of conduct disorder, they are not symptoms of "true" ADHD. Finally, Schuckit refers to these symptoms as "ADHD-type syndrome" as differentiated from "classical ADHD" (without conduct disorder) and concludes:

> Signs of hyperactivity along with a diminished attention span in childhood are associated with a variety of conditions. When these problems are related to conduct disorder, oppositional disorder, or are the temporary consequences of stresses in the home (perhaps related to parental alcoholism) then it is likely that the children

demonstrating an ADHD-type syndrome will have an enhanced future risk for alcohol dependence themselves. However, when a child demonstrates a classical ADHD condition in the absence of excessive aggressiveness or without fulfilling criteria for conduct oppositional disorders, there is no evidence that such individuals are at high risk for alcohol dependence. While not reviewed in depth here, similar conclusions can be drawn regarding the risk for abuse or dependence on drugs other than alcohol.[27]

While we respect the view of Schuckit, it is our contention that there is little or no evidence to demonstrate that ADHD, conduct disorder, and oppositional disorders are distinct disease entities. In fact, the research of David Comings suggests that these behaviors are all part of a "spectrum disorder."[28] As discussed earlier in this book, we believe that the above behaviors are indeed *not* separate disorders but are different expressions of the larger condition that we refer to as reward deficiency syndrome. In this case, it would be misleading to separate ADHD from conduct oppositional disorders when evaluating relationships between these behaviors and the risk for addiction.

Our position—that there is a relationship between ADHD, as part of reward deficiency syndrome, and the risk for substance use disorders—is supported by recent molecular genetic evidence that a number of dopamine variants (DRD2, DAT1, and DßH) associate across the wide spectrum of behavioral disorders such as ADHD, Tourette syndrome, and conduct disorder, as well as addictive behaviors, including alcoholism,[29] suggesting a common genetic anomaly.

It is also our opinion that the frustration and anger of undiagnosed, untreated, or misunderstood ADHD lead to symptoms that are labeled conduct disorder. If this is the case and if it is true that it is these symptoms that lead to addictive behavior, then it is urgent that we address and treat ADHD early, before serious life problems develop.

# 8

---

# Diagnosis of ADHD and Addiction

Confirming a diagnosis of attention deficit disorder and/or addiction is important for a number of reasons. The most important, perhaps, is the relief that comes with knowing for sure that there is a biological condition behind the behavior that has created the internal messages *I am bad* and *I am dumb*. Another is that accurate diagnosis can mean accurate treatment. Effective treatment methods are available, but until we know what we have, many are not options for us. Lack of diagnosis usually means lack of treatment. Complicating the picture is the fact that many people who suffer with ADHD also have other compulsive disorders, making the diagnosis difficult.

## DNA Testing

While there is not a test that will absolutely confirm the presence of ADHD or substance use disorders, there is good news regarding diagnosis. A test is now available that can determine whether a person has a predisposition for ADHD, substance use disorders, and other related behaviors. This test, in conjunction with other diagnostic measures, significantly increases the accuracy of a diagnosis of ADHD and substance use disorders.

Since the discovery relating alcoholism to the A1 allele of the D2 dopamine receptor gene, a number of great advances have taken place that have simplified DNA testing. Until recently DNA testing had to be performed either on blood or body tissue. However, Neu-Recovery International has developed a test for identifying the presence of the A1 allele of the dopamine D2 receptor gene by extracting DNA from cheek cells. This test, the first of its kind, simply involves swabbing the inside of the mouth—a noninvasive procedure. (This is good news for people who have needle phobia or low pain tolerance.) For information on how to get this DNA test see NeuRecovery International in the resource list at the end of the book.

To determine the presence of a gene indicating a predisposition for addiction, a single gene test is performed. While it has been determined mathematically that anyone who has the D2 receptor gene anomaly is at risk (as high as 70 percent) for a number of addictive behaviors, this does not mean that the affected person is doomed to a life of addiction. Likewise, not having the anomaly does not mean there is no risk at all of addiction because other genes, as yet unidentified, may be involved.

Since three dopaminergic genes that may be associated with attention deficit hyperactivity disorder have been identified, DNA testing involves the analysis of all three genes. The presence of more than one of these genes indicates an increased risk of having ADHD. Individuals having all three gene anomalies are at the highest risk of having ADHD and are likely to have it in a more severe form. If an individual does not carry any of the gene anomalies in the dopaminergic system, the likelihood of that person having ADHD is greatly diminished. However, not having any genetic anomaly does not mean the individual cannot have ADHD since other genes, still unidentified, may also cause a genetic predisposition. Certainly, combining the information of this test with other diagnostic tools to assess ADHD significantly increases the accuracy of the diagnosis.

## Confirming Diagnosis of ADHD

It is often a teacher who initiates the diagnostic process by informing parents that their child is daydreaming in class, failing to complete assignments, or driving everyone crazy with thoughtless behavior. It is usually from the diagnosis of their children that parents recognize their own symptoms and go through the diagnostic process themselves.

Diagnosis of ADHD should be done by a professional, usually a psychologist or a psychiatrist. It is important that actual assessment should be done by a person trained not only in recognizing ADHD but also conditions with similar symptoms in order to reduce the possibility that another serious condition may go untreated.

There are no blood tests or psychological tests that will absolutely confirm the presence of ADHD. It is, after all, a "behavioral" condition, meaning it is identified by behavioral criteria. To diagnose it we primarily look at behaviors we can see. However, there are a number of tests that can be used to rule out other conditions and to rule out or strongly suggest attention deficit hyperactivity disorder. Various professionals use various tests and we do not endorse any in particular. There are limitations to any diagnostic methods, but together many of them can make a strong case for a diagnosis of attention deficit hyperactivity disorder.

Most professionals diagnosing ADHD will use the criteria listed in a book called the *Diagnostic and Statistical Manual of Mental Disorders, Fourth Edition (DSM-IV)*. To be diagnosed using this criteria a person must have six or more symptoms from either of two lists of symptoms (or six from each list). The first is a list of symptoms indicating inattention, the second is a list of symptoms indicating hyperactivity and/or impulsivity.

*Symptoms of inattention:*

1. often fails to give close attention to details or makes careless mistakes in schoolwork, work, or other activities

2. often has difficulty sustaining attention in tasks or play activities and finds it hard to persist with tasks until completion

3. often does not seem to listen when spoken to directly

4. often does not follow through on instructions and fails to finish schoolwork, chores, or duties in the workplace (not due to oppositional behavior or failure to understand instructions)

5. often has difficulty organizing tasks or activities

6. often avoids, dislikes, or is reluctant to engage in tasks that require sustained mental effort (such as schoolwork or paperwork)

7. often loses things necessary for tasks or activities

8. often is distracted by extraneous stimuli

9. often is forgetful in daily activities

## Diagnosis of ADHD and Addiction

*Symptoms of hyperactivity or impulsivity:*

1. often fidgets with hands or feet or squirms in seat

2. often leaves seat in classroom or in other situations in which remaining seated is expected

3. often runs about or climbs excessively in situations in which it is inappropriate

4. often has difficulty playing or engaging in leisure activities quietly

5. often is on the go or often acts as if "driven by a motor"

6. often talks excessively

7. often blurts out answers before questions have been completed

8. often has difficulty awaiting turn or waiting in line

9. often interrupts or intrudes on others (e.g., butts into conversations or games)

These symptoms must have persisted for at least six months to a degree that is maladaptive and inconsistent with developmental level, some must have been present before the age of seven and present in more than one setting, and there must be clear evidence of impairment in social, academic, or occupational functioning.

Certainly, most experts would agree that to make a careful diagnosis one must eliminate other explanations for the symptoms. In this regard, the clinician should eliminate other problems such as anxiety, depression, and learning disorders. It should be remembered, however, that these problems can be symptoms of ADHD or conditions that coexist with ADHD. So their presence does not rule out ADHD. To distinguish these symptoms from ADHD or to determine whether they exist along with it, clinicians usually rely on interviews with parents and teachers, behavior-rating scales, and psychological tests.

### History

In determining whether someone has ADHD, the main objective, using the criteria we have listed from *Diagnostic and Statistical Manual, Fourth Edition (DSM-IV)*, is discovering how many symptoms the person has. But how do clinicians find out how many of the *DSM-IV* symptoms a person has? They ask the person and they ask other people who have observed the behavior of the person. They get a history of the problem. Usually symptoms of the condition have been present since early childhood, maybe before birth. Parents often will recall early symptoms that they at first associated with the child being especially energetic, curious, fussy, sensitive, or prone to temper outbursts.

Stories of impulsive behavior that goes beyond the impulsiveness of any normal child at any given age will be evaluated, as will indications of difficulty paying attention or sticking with an activity. You must remember, however, that all children have short attention spans and do impulsive things. That does not mean they have ADHD. Marilyn, who does not have ADHD, remembers at about four years old cutting a chunk right out of the front of her hair. This is a fairly common occurrence and exemplifies the normal impulsiveness that is part of childhood. Doug, however, remembers being told at about the same age not to touch the Creepy Crawler maker because it was hot and would burn him. Even knowing there probably would be painful consequences, he was overcome with an irresistible urge to touch it, and of course, he burned his fingers. This is the type of impulsive behavior associated with ADHD.

### School Performance

Much of the information about school performance needs to come from teachers. Some can come from grade cards and self-reports from the child. Some children exhibit symptoms of ADHD much more recognizably at school than at home. The extra stress and structure of the school setting may contribute to "acting out" of symptoms that may not be so apparent in other settings. The inability to obey rules, finish assignments, sit still, and follow directions will soon get most children into enough trouble that everyone around them is aware that school is difficult and painful for them. They may be considered daydreamers who can't stay with a project or assignment. They may be considered difficult children who need more self-control and discipline. But they will be noticed and there will be records and teachers' reports to confirm that this is a child with problems.

### Intelligence and Academic Performance

Intelligence and academic performance will be evaluated, but it is quite common for them to be inconsistent. While intelligence may be above normal, that will probably not be reflected in grades or records of academic achievement. This is a strong indicator that something is wrong and that it could be ADHD. The poor academic performance may be due to not following directions or not staying on task, but for some ADHD children—usually girls—it may be due to getting distracted by the details of the task itself.

Kathy: *Although there is ADHD in our family, we never thought that my daughter Cheryl had it. She was not hyperactive and did not seem to have difficulty focusing on a task. In fact, her problems in school stemmed from focusing too much. She was never able to finish her school work because she was so slow. She spent much of her recess time inside finishing assignments and never got to be "Top Banana" because her work was never finished. What she got done was always exceptionally well done but she received no validation for its quality because it was not finished. Teachers were always telling her to hurry, but she didn't know how to hurry. Whenever we told her to hurry she looked at us as if we were telling her to "hibblehob," and she had no context for knowing what that meant. We were surprised when she was diagnosed with ADHD, but medication allowed her to not only do a good job but to get the job finished. What was happening was that she could not stay focused on the goal of getting done. She was distracted by the details of the assignment. If she was to fill in some blanks and color some pictures on the same page, she got so distracted by coloring the pictures perfectly that she forgot all about filling in the blanks. Or if the teacher was dictating spelling words, Cheryl got so distracted by the need to have the word look good on the page that she was erasing and rewriting one word over and over, so she did not hear the next word. I was surprised that this was ADHD because the other people in my family with ADHD are unable to concentrate on one task and Cheryl seems to concentrate too much. Actually, it is just another form of distractibility.*

In adults, poor academic performance may be seen as the inability to finish college or a training program that could mean job advancement. Adults with ADHD may be working in jobs not in line with their interests or skills because they have never been able to stay with an educational program long enough to attain a degree, a certificate, or the training necessary for the work they would like to do.

## Medical Evaluation

It is important to consider and check out other causes of the symptoms that indicate ADHD. Sometimes allergies can mimic the symptoms. Because the symptoms can be similar, ADHD is sometimes treated as an allergy by eliminating certain foods. With true ADHD this may be a mistake, but if the symptoms are actually due to a food allergy, it is a mistake not to make the necessary adjustments in diet. Other neurological problems may also appear to be ADHD and should be ruled out. Epilepsy is a possibility.

> Patricia: *We were quite certain that Paul had ADHD, as were his teachers and his psychiatrist. His behavior was so bad he was isolated from his classmates most of the time not only so they could be freed of his problem behavior but so he could be freed from the stimulation of the classroom. His teacher began to notice, however, that sometimes he shook in a way that could not be accounted for if his problem was ADHD. She suggested that he have a thorough physical examination including an electroencephalogram (EEG). It turned out that Paul has a form of epilepsy. He is on the proper medication now and is like a new child. It has made a big difference, for him, our family, and his teachers, that we found out what was really wrong with him and did not continue looking for answers for a different problem.*

## Performance Tests

There are performance tests that can be used to assess a person's ability to focus attention and to refrain from impulsive actions. Two commonly used performance tests are the Matching Familiar Figures Test (MFFT)[1] and the Test of Variable Attention (TOVA).[2] In these tests the person responds to a "target" in a specified way and the responses are evaluated to determine how well the person is able to sustain attention and how often he or she responds impulsively (before adequate time to make the appropriate selection). While these tests can provide useful information, they are not 100 percent accurate and should only be considered along with other information.

### Brain Electrical Activity Mapping (BEAM)

Brain mapping is a technique that measures the electrical waves of the brain. Brain electrical activity can be observed and abnormalities identified. Electrical waves are generated when the brain performs specific tasks. The brain's response to external stimuli can be measured and is called evoked-response potential (ERP). The P300 component of ERP is a wave associated with information processing, attention, and memory. We have already mentioned that the amplitude of this wave is reduced in many alcoholics[3] and in sons of alcoholic fathers,[4] strongly confirming that these abnormalities are indeed predictors of a predisposition to alcoholism. (The brain electrical activity map allows a person trained to do so to detect this P300 abnormality.)

According to Eric Braverman and associates,[5] brain electrical activity mapping has important predictive value in identifying young children with ADHD. This further links a common abnormality involving brain electrical activity to both ADHD and substance use disorder. Kenneth Blum and Eric Braverman recently showed that the A1 allele dopamine D2 receptor gene is associated with a reduced response of the P300 wave.[6] We therefore suggest that the potential ADHD individual be evaluated with a brain map. For more information about brain mapping, contact Eric Braverman at Princeton Associates for Total Health (see Resources).

## Confirming Substance Use Disorders

As we have mentioned, there is now a DNA test that can confirm vulnerability to addiction. However, as with ADHD, there is no blood test or other infallible test to tell us that someone does or does not *currently* have a substance use disorder. It is necessary to gather information that tells a story and makes a case. In the *DSM-IV* there is criteria for making the decision once that information is gathered. For any addictive drug, *DSM-IV* gives criteria for diagnosing drug *dependence* or drug *abuse*.

In order to meet the criteria for *abuse* one must experience adverse consequences from use. These consequences may include problems with job performance or schoolwork, irresponsibility related to child care or family responsibilities, legal problems (such as driving while under the influence), medical problems, or other destructive behavior. Individuals who meet the criteria for alcohol abuse continue to use despite the knowledge that continued use poses significant problems for them and others.

In order to meet the criteria for *dependence*, one must experience a cluster of behavioral and physiological symptoms indicating that the person continues use of the substance despite problems. There is a pattern of repeated use that results in tolerance (needing more and more to get the effect), withdrawal (physical symptoms when the drug is not used), and compulsive drug-taking behavior.

Accurate assessment and diagnosis is the first step in learning to live with the conditions of ADHD and addiction and can make the difference between a life of frustration, shame, and guilt and a life of self-acceptance, appropriate treatment, and self-care.

> Cassie: *I felt reborn when I found out what had plagued me all my life. I still have many of the difficulties I had before—overreaction to noise, trouble concentrating, and impatience. But now I recognize what is happening and don't feel so bad about myself. I have learned how to reduce my stress and to react differently to situations that used to get me in trouble. There is no magic answer to this condition, but knowing what it is certainly is the first step to being able to live a better life in spite of it.*

# 9

## Treatment Options

**O**nce appropriate diagnosis of attention deficit hyperactivity disorder and/or substance use disorders has taken place, appropriate treatment must be selected. Treatment must fit the disorder. Throughout this book, we have shown that in a high number of cases, ADHD and addiction are the manifestation and outcome of neurochemical reward deficiency. It is for people who have this condition that we have written this book and for whom we address treatment options.

Reward deficiency means there is a deficiency in reward neurochemistry. Because deficiencies, excesses, or imbalances of "mellow molecules" directly relate to impulsive behaviors, high stress levels, intense anger, and attentional problems, it makes sense that if these stores are improved or balanced, the symptoms will at least improve. Introducing healthy alternatives constitutes good treatment for this condition.

When we use the term treatment we mean any help given by any qualified clinician in any number of settings. Help is usually extended through various modalities of care such as individual counseling, medication, educational instruction, group counseling, individual assignment-oriented activities, and support groups.

The first requirement for recovery is *abstinence from mind-altering chemicals and behaviors* used as self-medication. This does not mean a person cannot take nonaddictive prescribed medication (if used as prescribed). But continued use of a substance or behavior that allows the addiction cycle to develop or continue interferes with learning healthier ways of living.

The second requirement for recovery is learning about the physiological foundation of ADHD and addiction in order to (1) personally relate to the symptoms, (2) have a basis upon which to make treatment choices, and (3) have the knowledge to take appropriate lifelong care of oneself. Often, the most profound changes begin when people are able to see that there is a condition that directly relates to the dysfunction and pain they have experienced. They are not defective or bad. They simply have a physiological condition that creates different ways of feeling, thinking, perceiving, and living life. And even though these perceptions often interfere with life, treatment should help the person understand how these unique perceptions also identify their creative talents and specialness.

The third requirement for recovery is learning to live differently. Old ways of coping may no longer be appropriate or effective. Destructive ways of coping must be replaced with healthy ways of coping. Because some people with ADHD have learning disabilities, it may be difficult for them to make the many adjustments that recovery requires. In addition, change is difficult. It is not easy to give up compensatory behaviors; even though they have had negative consequences, they have also helped. Part of recovery, then, is finding resources to support change.

## Choosing Professional Helpers

In choosing a professional to serve as a guide to recovery from ADHD and/or addiction, it is acceptable to be selective. Because a person with a reward deficiency has higher than normal stress levels and brings into recovery overwhelming shame, it is essential that the treatment environment be as peaceful, caring, nurturing, and safe as possible. While there is much work to accomplish in the framework of treatment, it can be an enjoyable and rewarding experience.

Be wary of a professional who makes a diagnosis of ADHD, gives a prescription for medication, and sends you on your way. It may be necessary to have a treatment *team* in order to receive all the aspects of treatment required for full recovery. Taking a pill, even if that is part of treatment, is not all there is to recovery. People with ADHD and addiction should be learning *how* to live. They should be developing the skills to experience pleasure without using mood-altering substances. They should be learning better life management skills than they have used in the past. They should be learning to utilize the good aspects of ADHD in creative ways. This requires more than a pill.

Be wary also of treatment professionals who use—or recommend that others use—harsh confrontation to motivate behavior change. Whether dealing with ADHD or addiction, harsh confrontation will only aggravate the symptoms. Attempting to "confront" someone out of the symptoms will only allow for the strengthening of the normal defense systems. Shame will interfere with, rather than aid, recovery. Shaming the person further with harsh confrontation will not only complicate the disorder but directly contribute to more pain and anger, and ultimately more failure.

## Choosing Treatment Methods

Treatment should provide healthy, alternative solutions for feeling better. It should provide an initial period of learning that begins with the diagnostic discovery and continues on through the treatment process into lifelong self-care. Treatment should provide the healthy choices available to reduce the severity of symptoms of ADHD and heal or prevent the pain of addiction.

From the present research it cannot be assumed that any one treatment method works for all people or for all symptoms of any one person. We must look instead at using as many different methods as feasible in order to feel better. Even though you are using many different treatment approaches successfully, you will still no doubt have some periodic discomfort. This is a lifelong condition. Treatment merely treats the symptoms; it does not cure the condition. That's why the next chapter is about self-care—what you can do on an ongoing basis to live as comfortably and productively as possible.

A main objective of early recovery is to provide enough relief to prevent a return to old addictive methods of pain relief or the development of other substitute addictive behaviors. It is important to remember that as long as addictive use continues, effective treatment, healthy self-care, and full recovery is not possible. Although they may fall short of providing the "instant" relief that addictive chemicals provide, an assortment of treatment remedies are available for a comfortable transition into a happy and healthy life.

## Medication for Attention Deficit Hyperactivity Disorder

Medication is the most common treatment for ADHD. This should not be interpreted to mean that it is the only treatment, the best treatment, or that it is appropriate for everyone that has ADHD. While it is certainly an option, it should not be the exclusive treatment used by anyone and for many people it perhaps should not be used at all. It is a matter of controversy whether or not a person recovering from an addiction should use any medication. While we do not take a firm position on this matter, we do believe it is very important for people who are recovering to be very careful about any medication they take. They should be aware of the effects and side effects of anything they try. If there is any significant feeling of being high or euphoric or if tolerance builds (you need more and more to get the effect), then we suggest it is not wise for a recovering person to continue taking that medication.

Medication should only be given under medical supervision and after the proper diagnosis. Because there are numerous other problems that have similar symptoms and coexist with ADHD, careful monitoring of medication by a professional who is familiar with all these conditions—*including addiction*—is essential.

Medication, in many cases, has proved helpful in reducing the severity of the symptoms of ADHD. But it is certainly no cure-all. For some people it works wonders; for others it may produce no improvement at all. For some sufferers medication brings relief but is not worth the side effects. Even if the medication has dramatic effects and significantly improves the quality of one's life, it still does not cure the disorder; it only modifies the symptoms.[1] Two of the most common types of medications prescribed for ADHD are stimulants and tricyclic antidepressants.[2]

## Stimulants

The stimulants usually prescribed are Ritalin (the generic name is methylphenidate), Dexedrine (dextroamphetamine), and Cylert (pemoline). Through the stimulation of the central nervous system by these drugs, the person can focus better and often experience improved mood. Some common side effects may be suppression of appetite, loss of sleep, elevated heart rate and blood pressure, nausea, and headaches (which usually subside in a few days).[3]

> Mike: *Ritalin helped me the most by helping me to focus. It's like looking down a pair of binoculars with your brain. Everything is kind of fuzzy until you adjust the center wheel. Taking Ritalin is like adjusting the binoculars. Everything clicks into focus. Instead of darting around the room so much I look at what I want to look at. My thinking slips into gear and I am able to follow a steady process.*

We suggest, however, that Ritalin be taken cautiously. There are a number of potential problems that may be associated with its use. There are increasing reports of Ritalin abuse and overuse. There are no good long-term studies on its use. So we are not sure what the long-term effects may be. Sometimes if a child's behavior improves he or she may be forced to continue taking it, even though the child complains of adverse effects. Children should be listened to about their reactions to it, and what they say should be taken seriously.

Perhaps the point of most concern is the fact that with its widespread acceptance, doctors prescribe it and parents accept the prescription without looking for other possible options for their children. Some people on Ritalin feel that, while reducing their hyperactivity and impulsiveness, it takes away their creativity and spontaneity. A variety of possibilities should be explored before assuming that Ritalin—or any medication for that matter—is the only option. Other, more "natural" treatments may reduce the unpleasant symptoms while not taking away the traits that may be part of the person's natural personality.

While Ritalin is sometimes also prescribed for adults with ADHD, the published literature on the treatment of adults does not present overwhelming evidence of efficacy.[4] In discussing the abuse potential of Ritalin, mixed feelings surface. Although there is little recorded evidence that adults treated with these drugs become dependent on them, the drugs themselves have a history as substances of abuse and we believe it is appropriate to be cautious about treatment with stimulants, especially when there is a history of stimulant abuse. Some people also experience adverse side effects or reactions to Ritalin.

> Brad: *I had been addicted to crack cocaine. When I was diagnosed with ADHD my doctor thought Ritalin would probably help me, but I had a very bad reaction to it. I felt like I was coming out of my skin. I felt very agitated and anxious.*

There is another case to be made for being cautious about the use of Ritalin for either children or adults. There is strong evidence of a genetic link between ADHD and Tourette syndrome and the two often occur together. Anyone with Tourette syndrome should not take a stimulant since stimulants can cause or exacerbate tics that are common with Tourette syndrome.[5] This is another reason why a thorough evaluation should be done before medication is prescribed.

### Antidepressants

Another type of medication used to treat ADHD is tricyclic antidepressant medication. This includes Norpramin (the generic name is desipramine), Pamelor (nortriptyline), and Tofranil (imipramine).[6] Although these drugs are very different from Ritalin, they work to increase the amount of dopamine and norepinephrine in the synapse and the effects on the symptoms of ADHD are similar. Some side effects of these drugs include dry mouth, dizziness (especially upon standing quickly), lowering of blood pressure, constipation, and mild urinary retention.[7]

Usually there is no way to know what medication would be best for someone other than through trial and error. There are some things to consider, though, that may influence the direction to proceed. Whereas with Ritalin the effects are immediate, often it takes time—perhaps a couple of weeks—to experience the effects of antidepressants. One disadvantage to using Ritalin is that its effects wear off within hours after it is taken and there are varying degrees of effectiveness between doses. However, twice-a-day use of an antidepressant produces an even effect throughout the day. This regimen is recommended by Dr. Hans Huessy, who prefers it over the use of Ritalin.[8]

While we recognize that many benefit from the use of medication for ADHD, we also want to point out that there are always risks and unknown effects to any drug that alters functioning of the brain. The neurochemical balance is very delicate and we don't know in most cases how taking a drug for a specific neurochemical effect may alter other neurochemical interactions. Also, no one really knows the long-term consequences of regular use of a drug such as Ritalin. We therefore recommend utilizing solutions other than medication when those can be found.

## Medication for Addiction

Antabuse (disulfiram) is a drug sometimes used to deter drinking. It does not abolish the craving or desire to drink. It simply makes you deathly sick if alcohol is consumed while the drug is in the system. The drug blocks normal liver enzyme activity after the conversion of alcohol to acetaldehyde. This causes excessive accumulation of acetaldehyde, which is toxic, and produces symptoms of intense flushing and warming of the face, a severe throbbing headache, shortness of breath, chest pains, nausea, repeated vomiting, sweating, and weakness.[9] In other words, Antabuse works to deter drinking by the reaction that occurs if someone drinks while using it. It can be effective in preventing impulse drinking and can be beneficial in helping people stay abstinent while they learn sobriety skills. But use of Antabuse is not a long-term cure and is not effective treatment by itself.

Naltrexone, a pure opioid antagonist, partially or completely blocks the subjective effects of opiates for as long as twenty-four hours. If the dose is doubled, it will block the effects for forty-eight hours; if tripled, for seventy-two hours. The FDA has just approved using it, under the brand name ReVia for treatment of alcoholism. It makes drinking much less pleasurable and reduces relapse.[10]

Our opinion about medication for substance disorders is the same as it is about medications for ADHD. They should not be the only form of treatment used. They are only aids to recovery, not cures. But they may be very effective in providing one form of support as a part of total treatment.

## Neuronutrients

Kenneth Blum was instrumental in developing neuronutrient formulations of ingredients to produce a more balanced brain chemistry. These neuronutrients are the result of over twenty-five years of research, development, and testing. They are designed to provide the proper amounts of vitamins, amino acids, and minerals essential for proper brain nutrition.

Different formulations were developed for various conditions: one for those who may have been addicted to depressant drugs like alcohol, another for those who may have been addicted to stimulant drugs such as cocaine, and still another for those who have attempted to medicate their reward deficiency by overeating. David Miller has found it effective himself and recommends it to clients with ADHD who, in most cases, find it very beneficial. For more information on neuronutrients contact NeuRecovery International (see Resources).

Neuronutrients can provide the brain a nutritional buffet from which it selects what it needs to restore balance. These supplements are scientifically formulated and have shown through thousands of cases that symptoms of reward deficiency can be relieved by using them. They, of course, are not a cure-all. Nothing is. But neuronutrients, along with better nutrition, can restore some healthy brain chemistry and produce some positive behavioral responses. They can be used in addition to medication or instead of medication in some cases.

Mil: *I have taken neuronutrients for over eight years with much success. My temperament is improved and my hypervigilance modified. Many of my recovering friends also take them and are happy with the results. I have tried numerous prescription medications for my ADHD but none has helped me as much as the neuronutrients. Well, some helped the ADHD, but living with the side effects was not worth it for me. I have no adverse side effects from the neuronutrients.*

For many people, even those who have not been addicted, the neuronutrients have been found to be very beneficial in controlling symptoms of ADHD.

Julie: *I am very impressed with the results I have had from the neuronutrients. For me they are much better than Ritalin. Ritalin tends to give me an artificial sense of well-being, whereas the neuronutrients just help me feel in balance. I am working on diet and behavior modification to control my ADHD, but when I use the neuronutrients, a strict diet is not as necessary to maintain the needed balance within my system. This is helpful when traveling or eating out. Even though I am not recovering from any addiction, I have certainly had good results from this product.*

## Brain Wave Biofeedback

When hearing of biofeedback, some people think of fad therapy. This may be because of some past claims for it as a cure-all for whatever ailed you. Biofeedback, however, has been found effective in the treatment of a wide variety of conditions. What this technology does is give feedback about biological conditions of which we usually are not consciously aware—heart rate, body temperature, muscle tenseness, and skin response. With this feedback we can learn to alter biological states: decrease heart rate, raise body temperature, relax muscle tension. While it is not a magic cure for high blood pressure, migraine headaches, and stress-related conditions, it has been found to be an effective adjunct to other treatments for these conditions.

With computerized technology, we now can use this therapy to produce *brain wave* feedback. In an earlier chapter, we discussed the fact that people with ADHD often show a brain wave pattern that is recognizably different from "normal" in that there is an excess of theta waves and a deficit of beta waves. Theta waves are relatively slow in frequency and accompany deep reverie or a daydreaming, unfocused state. Beta waves are higher in frequency and demonstrate focus and attention.

It makes sense then that since most people with ADHD are more detached and less focused, they have an overabundance of theta waves. Specialists in the use of biofeedback for ADHD are presently studying the differences in brain waves between people who have attention deficit with hyperactivity and those without.

To show the brain waves on the computer, several electrodes are attached (with paste) to the scalp at various locations. Through auditory and visual feedback, one can learn either to inhibit or enhance certain types of brain waves. The brain can be "reconditioned" to regulate the brain wave irregularities. It has been demonstrated that often with sufficient treatments (usually twenty-five to thirty-five thirty-minute sessions) people with ADHD can learn to significantly inhibit theta waves and enhance beta waves and thus experience greater clarity of thought and higher energy levels. Over time these brain wave changes have been shown to continue even without further treatments.[11] Shown here is the brain wave pattern of one person before and after biofeedback training.

---

These graphs show the results of twenty brain wave biofeedback sessions with a female age forty-eight with ADHD. The graphs show the amplitude of theta and beta waves over time (one minute). The top lines represent theta and the bottom lines represent beta. Notice in the first graph the space between theta and beta and the spikes in the theta. This is the client's first brain wave biofeedback training session. The second graph is her twentieth session. Notice the interwoven pattern of theta and beta. Also, theta never goes above three microvolts. In graph one it goes up to ten microvolts. The scale on the second graph is half the range of the first to show more detail.

# Treatment Options

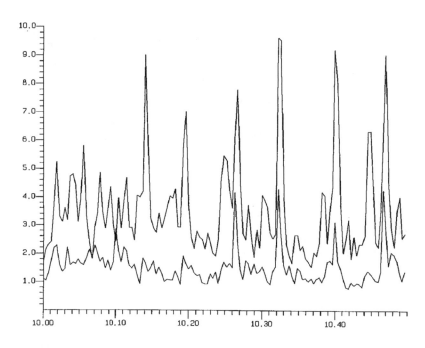

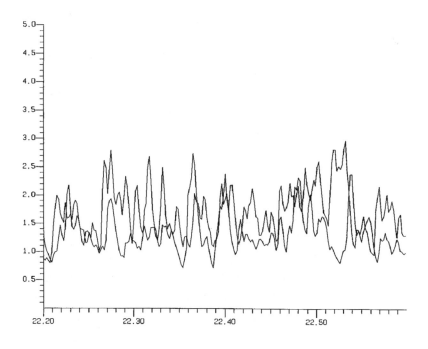

It is important to note at this point that if a person recovering from addiction does not have attention deficit hyperactivity disorder or has ADHD without the excess of theta waves common with ADHD, that a different brain wave biofeedback method may be appropriate. Alcoholics without attention deficit hyperactivity disorder sometimes have an excess of beta waves (the attention waves) and can benefit from brain wave biofeedback procedures that inhibit beta waves. *For this reason it is very important for every recovering addict or alcoholic to be assessed for attention deficit hyperactivity disorder before using brain wave biofeedback.* People with excess theta waves need to learn to enhance beta waves and should not be learning to inhibit them.

### Cranial Electrical Stimulation

Cranial Electrical Stimulation (CES) provides a small, gentle electrical current that stimulates the production of brain chemicals that increase a feeling of well-being.[12] CES provides its stimulation through the placement of two electrodes, usually on the lower portions of the jaw area. Some clinicians apply the electrodes to the head and the wrist. CES works through the use of a pocket-size unit that easily can be carried from place to place.

Some studies indicate that low-voltage electrical stimulation of the brain is therapeutically beneficial in the treatment of conditions such as depression, substance use disorder, withdrawal symptoms, and insomnia.[13] CES produces an increase in beta-endorphin levels and acetylcholine levels, which blocks anxiety and improves cognitive functioning. It can directly affect the stress levels connected with a reward deficiency by producing more relaxing, reward-enhancing brain chemistry.

CES has also been shown to significantly improve the P300 brain wave,[14] which of course has been associated with ADHD as it relates to both drug craving and attention span. Braverman and his associates have shown through brain mapping that many serious disorders of the brain have electrical rhythm disturbances. CES may normalize a variety of these rhythm disturbances.[15] While it is a relatively unknown treatment option, it is gaining clinical recognition for its effectiveness.

Sue: *I get so much relief from the CES experience. It relaxes me and helps me feel in control and in balance. It is a very pleasant experience. It reduces my stress and also the desire to get high with drugs.*

A doctor's prescription is necessary for a CES instrument. For more information, contact Eric Braverman at Princeton Associates for Total Health (see Resources).

### Acupuncture

Acupuncture therapy has been used for thousands of years. It stimulates pain-blocking neurochemistry through the exact placement of very fine needles. Sometimes the needles are merely put in place and sometimes they are manipulated. Acupuncture recently has been tried as a treatment approach for substance use disorders. While studies showing outcomes are as yet inconclusive, some practitioners report good results.

Evidence of beneficial results is strong enough to suggest that this therapy deserves consideration as a treatment approach for both ADHD and addiction. It is relatively inexpensive and has not been found to be harmful (although care should be taken to ensure that needles are always adequately sterilized to avoid the spread of AIDS, hepatitis, and other diseases). As with other approaches mentioned, the treatment should be provided under the care of a trained professional, along with other treatments known to be beneficial.

## Skills Training

Because people with ADHD don't have internal structure, it is especially important for them to have external structure. Structure provides limits that reduce inner chaos and increase a sense of control. Structure provides boundaries within which people with ADHD can function more productively, as well as express their creativity and abilities. They must utilize everything they can to be able to work smarter and not quite as hard or self-defeatingly. But most of them don't know how to go about structuring their lives. If they knew how, they already would be doing it.

We suggest life management skills classes, preferably with other people with the same problem and with an instructor who understands the problem. It is helpful to learn to use tools such as appointment books, schedules, and list making. If a class isn't available, we suggest a coach that will help set up some organizational plans and support the ADHD person in practicing the skills until they become habits.

> Del: *Something that has helped me build brakes into my life is keeping a schedule. Writing down what I'm supposed to do and when helps me keep a routine. It helps me look at my day in segments. When I look at sections of time—from this time to that time—I am better able to put on brakes because I know when it is time to stop. And I know when to go on to the next activity. I know that sounds awfully simple and maybe a little foolish, but I need [the schedule in order] to know when something is going to begin and when it is going to end.*

Remember, however, that it is possible to become compulsive about organization. This is how some people cope, but that can be a problem too. It is best to try to stay only as organized as you need to be. Simplification is sometimes the truly important aspect of organization for a person with ADHD. Sometimes it is appropriate to apply the four Ds: drop, delay, delegate, and do. This may sound deadly for an ADHD person, but it involves dropping anything that is not really important, especially anything that interferes with what is really important; delaying what can wait while taking care of what needs to be done right away; delegating to someone else whatever can be delegated without taking advantage of others; and doing what really needs to be done when it needs to be done.

### Study Skills

People with ADHD can usually benefit from some instruction and guidance in adopting effective study skills. They need skills that will enable them to focus as constructively as possible. They need to learn to break down learning into small, manageable pieces of information instead of large bites that overwhelm. There are skills that can be learned and practiced that will facilitate learning: taking notes, using tape recordings that can be replayed to fill in blanks missed by lack of concentration, setting a time and place to study. New study skills will foster confidence and assurance in the ability to learn. If new skills are learned and a sense of control is gained, the fear and shame connected with education may gradually be replaced with the confidence and excitement that should go with learning.

## Social Skills

Lack of confidence leads to poor social skills. Lack of confidence is a normal reaction to being asked over and over again, "Why did you do that?" And, "Why did you say that?" Or, "Why can't you behave?" Or, "Why don't you pay attention?" Not knowing how to explain themselves, people with ADHD learn to keep feelings in until they can contain them no longer and blow up. This anger that accompanies ADHD interferes with relationship building.

Those with ADHD often cannot sit still or stay comfortably in the present long enough to listen attentively. Their impulsivity causes problems with others who may be the recipients of impulsive actions. Since so many people with ADHD have come to expect negative reactions from others, a certain distrust may develop. They move away from others into isolation, and thus away from productive social functioning.

Part of recovery is learning new social skills. There are classes available for teaching these skills. Social skills are learned by practice and it is never too late to unlearn habits that have interfered with good relationships and learn new skills that will facilitate building better ones. In addition, assertiveness skills and anger control classes may be helpful.

## Vocational Counseling

Job hopping and lost jobs are common life problems for those with ADHD. Job or career counseling may be invaluable in learning the skills to keep a job or to find more satisfying work. Counseling to prepare for a job more in line with undeveloped or unused talents and abilities may be an important step in overcoming the limitations that coping with ADHD has imposed. Having ADHD does not mean settling for less. Learning what restrictions go with ADHD is not the same thing as settling for mediocrity. Knowing our restrictions simply enables us to live more freely within our limits as we learn to adjust to them.

## Special Considerations

People with ADHD need to be given special consideration and sometimes allowances should be made. In the home and in the classroom, accommodations can be made to reduce distractions for children. Children can be offered special understanding and support. More recently, adults with ADHD are beginning to seek special treatment. Under the 1990 Americans with Disabilities Act, they can insist upon help in the workplace and even in higher education. In universities and in medical schools, students diagnosed with ADHD are assisted by lengthened time for exam taking. And in the workplace, offices are being equipped with white-noise machines to reduce distractions.

The special considerations necessary for a person with ADHD should not be thought of as enabling irresponsible behavior even if the person is also addicted. In the addiction field it is helpful in breaking through the denial of people with substance use disorders to allow them to experience the full consequences of their behavior by refusing to protect them or to do for them things they should do for themselves. To do otherwise is thought of as *enabling* addictive behavior.

Addicted people need to be allowed to take responsibility for their own behavior and the same is true of people with ADHD. Having ADHD or addiction is not an excuse to be irresponsible, and, ultimately, we all have to be responsible for ourselves. But when dealing with people with these disorders we must remember that for a person with ADHD what may seem like unwillingness to behave in what others consider a responsible manner may in reality be an *inability* to do so. As Dr. Hans Huessy says, "ADHD is a lack of self-control on a biochemical basis."[16]

> Sue: *I was on the phone talking to my six-year-old grandson (who has ADHD) about school (where he has endless problems). I asked him if he was trying to be good and he said, "Well, Grandma, I don't try to be bad."*

When dealing with adolescents, this can be an especially difficult dilemma. When problems with an ADHD adolescent arise, adults are tempted, and often encouraged, to use "tough love." The consequences of this approach should be considered very carefully. Young people who have not yet learned the skills to cope with ADHD, given the choice to "shape up or ship out," may have no choice but to ship out because they do not know how to shape up. And they are ill-equipped to ship out and take complete responsibility for their own lives. It is best for a family to seek every option and every source of help before resorting to a "tough love" choice that can result in devastating consequences. Tough love is usually not appropriate for a person with an ADHD diagnosis, unless there is a delicate balance maintained between "tough" and "love" and unless the potential consequences of "tough" are considered very carefully.

# 10

## Self-Care

We are not responsible for our reward deficiency or ADHD, but we are responsible for what we do about it. We cannot use it as an excuse to live compulsively, impulsively, or addictively. Most of us who are affected by this chronic, often debilitating, condition inherited it and are not to blame for the symptoms. But once we know what we have and can see how it has affected our lives, we have a responsibility to do something about it. Through diagnosis, education, and treatment we have gained a better idea of what we are dealing with. We may get professional help, but ultimately it is up to us to use what we have learned and make choices that will enable us to live better.

Attention deficit hyperactivity disorder and the reward deficiency behind it are conditions that require self-management. Self-care is what we do for ourselves on a regular day-to-day basis to take care of ourselves. What we have is not a disorder that is treated and then fixed once and for all. We always have it. Even if it improves with medication, neuronutrients, or brain wave biofeedback, we still have it. We must learn—whether we are adults or children, whether we are recovering from addiction or preventing addiction—to take special measures that other people may not find necessary. A neurochemical deficiency is what we have; self-care is what we do to manage it. It is not what we do merely to cope; it is what we do to live fully and productively.

### The "I Can"

by David

Somewhere in the deep of me is the "I can,"
its should-be-crystal-clear voice stifled by layers

of cruddy doubt sitting on its sparkle all these years,
darkening its shining face,
blinding its wondrous eyes to beauty's form.

Always there is this "I can," even though in stuporous sleep
its thin voice wasted, dormant, unused.
Sometimes, for whatever reason,
some truth penetrates its thick wall of doubt,
energizing hope that all may yet be,
that all may not be lost,
that the "I can" will.

Self-care is a day-to-day, year-to-year, lifelong endeavor. It is learning to work and live smarter and creatively. It is moving into healthy living out of an impulsive, compulsive, addictive way of life. It is living a wholesome, balanced lifestyle. Everyone should live this way. But some people can get by with less and not experience the same negative consequences. We cannot.

Unless we are constantly choosing healthier foods, healthier thoughts, healthier activities, we are in danger of reverting back to the unhealthy, counterproductive, destructive living we are attempting to move away from. For us, the consequences of not living healthfully and productively are dire.

Since change is so very difficult for those with ADHD, life in recovery demands a program of self-care that will enable us to deal with the stresses of a changing lifestyle. Even though the old lifestyle of addiction was destructive and created many problems, it was predictable. It was like an old, comfortable pair of jeans, ragged and full of holes and really not serving us too well anymore but in which we felt a certain comfort and security. Habits provide comfort because they are familiar, and breaking these old habits will be difficult. But remember, self-care is more than stopping old behaviors; it is learning to replace the old habits with new ones. The transition is aided when these new habits are perceived as enjoyable. The following suggestions may help to make them so:

1. Find an enjoyable behavior to replace the undesirable one. Don't merely try to "stop."

2. Practice the new behavior frequently as a method of relearning.

3. Avoid risky situations likely to lead back to the old behavior.

4. Ask others for help and support.

5. Be realistic; allow sufficient time for relearning.

6. A mistake is not failure; learn from mistakes.

Remember, we are in charge of our own lives. If other people or circumstances are perceived to be in charge, then we are giving away what power we have. We can change. And we are well worth the effort and courage to change what we can. A lifestyle of recovery demands that we adjust to new thoughts, feelings, activities, friends, and, most of all, to ourselves. We don't have to do this all at once. Only by taking one step at a time can we make the changes we need to make on the road to recovery.

> There was once a young farm boy whose father was away and whose mother asked him to go to the barn in the dark to feed the animals. But he was afraid of the dark. His mother assured him that the lantern would furnish the light he needed to get there and back. "But the lantern only shines its light a short way in front of me," he said. "I can't see all the way to the barn." Then handing him the lantern, his mother took him outside. "Now, son," she said, "just take one step toward the barn." As he took one step the light moved ahead of him. "All you have to do," his mother told him, "is take one step at a time and the light will go before you all the way."[1]

## Twelve-Step Programs

People who have ADHD and people recovering from addiction need the support of other people who have the same conditions. People recovering from both especially need this support. The best source of this support that we know of is a twelve-step program such as Alcoholics Anonymous or Narcotics Anonymous.

The program of these groups and the twelve steps that they are based on provide guidelines for a new way of life centered around acceptance, honesty, and reaching out to others. They offer—through a proven path taken by many before us—a way and means for making right changes at the right times. They are based on members sharing their experience and what has worked best for them. These self-help groups are worldwide fellowships of men and women who help each other maintain sobriety and who offer to share their recovery experience freely with others who may have a drinking problem, other drug problem, or an addictive behavior.

Despite the fact that many thousands of people have achieved sobriety through their participation in these self-help groups, many have come to recognize that they also require professional counseling or treatment. Self-help groups are concerned solely with personal recovery and continuing sobriety of individuals who turn to them for help. They do not engage in research or medical or psychiatric treatment and do not endorse any causes, although members may individually participate in other organizations. They have adopted a policy of "cooperation but not affiliation" with other organizations concerned with the problem of addiction.

These organizations are places where we can meet friends with whom we can feel safe and comfortable in new and healthy ways as we attempt to understand our disorder and share with those who are in the same boat.

The twelve steps, because they were fashioned into lifestyle guidelines by those who needed to live by them, have become the single most effective type of treatment for addictions. The steps themselves are spiritually based rather than religiously. They offer simple, straightforward guidelines for moving into right relationships with ourselves, others, and a higher power that we define for ourselves.

## Coping with Stimulus Augmentation (Overload)

Overload, high distractibility, hypervigilance, and stimulus augmentation all mean principally the same thing. When a person's filtering system does not work well, perception is altered. We cannot do anything about the fact that some of us process the world's reality this way. But again, we are responsible for doing what we can to make it more tolerable. We can learn to soften our environment, separate ourselves periodically from unpleasant noises and sensations.

> David: *I may leave home without my American Express card. But I will never leave home without my earplugs! One of the best gifts of my life was a pair of earplugs given to me by a friend that works for General Motors. They have ridges on them that fit comfortably and snugly into the ear and, best of all, they work great. I can still hear with them in, but they soften the noise quite a bit so at least my nervous system doesn't spasm when that "no muffler" car roars by.*

We can take steps to gain more control. In addition to earplugs, a "white-noise" machine might be a good choice. These wonderful little gadgets emit a soft, masking sound like a waterfall, an ocean, or similar sound and cover up those clanging, banging noises. Also, a fan or a computer may work because they both emit white noise of their own. Some people leave on the fan to their central air or heat to give them constant white noise. Many of us are truly fans of fans.

There are things that can be done, too, where we live or spend time to quiet the environment. Double-paned glass doors or windows and carpeting on the floor—or even carpeting on the wall—can deaden sound and allow some protection from unwanted sound intrusions. Learn to lower the noise levels in your environment. Tone down the music and turn off the television once in a while. The environment can also be softened with music; overstuffed furniture; simple, "pleasant-to-the-eye" decor; and harmonious colors.

> Anne: *I used to watch television to help me to shut off my brain. But when I watched the news or a TV program, it seemed to disquiet my mind, and I would go to sleep more agitated. When I moved to Hawaii, I didn't take my TV with me. What I've learned is that TV did not shut off my brain—it gave me more things to think about.*
>
> *My apartment now is very quiet. Not having that noise on makes a big difference. I feel more calm and relaxed without TV in my life. It has made all the difference in the world. It's as if the quietness has helped me to find an off button. I'm really at peace here. I feel centered and I like that.*

We can learn to separate ourselves periodically from the crowded stimuli we live with. We can put a DO NOT DISTURB sign on the door.

We can make time for quiet activities like browsing the libraries, bookstores, museums. Or we can seek the quiet places in the great outdoors. In these ways we temporarily can eliminate noisy, chaotic activities.

> Gale: *Something that has often helped me is to go to a hot tub or a swimming pool where I float on my back. With my ears just under the water, I hear a roaring sound. The act of floating this way and the white noise that the water creates in my head relaxes and calms me and slows down my thought processes. I had a similar reaction when I went to the tanning beds. The warmth and the white noise of the hum of the tanning bed helped shut out my noise.*

But there are good sounds going on in the world, right along with the obnoxious ones. Most of the time, sounds of children playing and laughing can be pleasant. These playful sounds of life can be some of the greatest sounds of all, the sounds of living.

The perception of touch is also affected by stimulus augmentation. Letting people know to what extent you are comfortable being touched is important. It is also important to be comfortable physically with comfortable shoes and clothes.

> Robin: *Something that has helped me a lot with my stimulus augmentation is wearing comfortable clothing. When I have tight or poor-fitting clothes on, my stress levels go way up. It's not something most people think of as mattering when we talk about changing our environment. But it does make a difference.*

## Physical Exercise

Our bodies were designed to be in motion. And physical exercise increases the production of those "mellow molecules" that reduce pain levels and help us feel better. Exercise alters brain chemistry, offsets cravings, helps us relax, and provides vitality for a new lifestyle. Even though exercise is often associated with drudgery and pain, it can be fun and enjoyable. It can add pleasure and free us from the pain and discomfort that so often accompanies neurochemical reward deficiency.

Moving encourages moving. The more we move—however we do it—the better we feel and the more energy we have. It provides a safety valve for stress, helps with weight management, lowers blood sugar, strengthens the heart, increases energy, and improves sleep. We feel enlivened when we move. Movement allows us to feel our muscles work, our heart beat, and the blood flow through our body, creating energy and a feeling of well-being.

Whether we choose to walk, jog, swim, dance, or bicycle, these are aerobic ways to reduce stress and give us a lift. It's important to engage in exercise that we enjoy because otherwise we will not stick with it. It is also important to have alternatives. Swimming is a wonderful and sensuous way to exercise. Unfortunately, it is also more difficult to accomplish because most people do not own pools and must go to a health club to do it. And many people with ADHD are too disorganized to get there on a regular basis. Health clubs are often noisy, too, and a bit chaotic.

Walking may be the easiest and requires the least equipment. All one needs is a good pair of walking shoes and the time and space to do it. Many people walk in shopping malls because it may be safer and certainly can be warmer in winter and cooler in summer. But crowded shopping malls may not inspire anything but dread in overstimulated people. Conversely, a walk in the park can be not only invigorating but inspiring as well. As we become part of a quieter, more peaceful environment, we often can open up to the natural connections around us. Natural sounds are usually harmonious and easy on the ear and soul.

## Nutrition

Since nutrition is directly related to brain chemistry formation and synthesis, it is essential to proper self-care to learn what substances produce chemical payoffs and reward. Neurotransmitters are produced from amino acids, the building blocks of proteins. Some foods have an abundance of certain vitamins, amino acids, and minerals; some do not. Also, certain foods produce certain reactions. High sugar and caffeine, for instance, can produce erratic stress levels. High-protein foods (chicken, fish, lean meat, beans, milk products) can create more alertness. On the other hand, high-carbohydrate foods (potatoes, pasta, bread, rice) can produce relaxation. So one can learn to eat higher protein foods earlier in the day to promote more focusing ability and eat higher carbohydrate content in the evening to promote relaxation and restful sleep.

Since people with ADHD lack the biochemical balance to deal effectively with stress, learning which foods increase stress and which reduce it is an essential part of physically caring for ourselves. Once good nutrition has begun, the payoff will be motivation to continue good nutritional habits. Sometimes nutritional intake can make the difference between a good day and a disaster. But one must learn what foods produce what results. Some of this will be learned by trial and error because we all have different nutritional needs depending upon our individual neurochemical cascade differences.

Through better nutrition we can begin to see how dramatically emotions and feelings can change for the better. Eating certain foods may produce immediate pleasure or relief but can, in the long run, have damaging effects on brain chemical levels (as well as overall health). Eating large amounts of food high in fat may, for example, produce brain chemistry changes that create pleasant short-term feelings. But over time, a diet disproportionately high in fats may deprive the brain of an adequate supply of other nutrients necessary for balanced brain chemistry.

We can take the initiative to read and study labels on food packages. The stakes are too high not to take the initiative! By learning to eat the right foods, we are learning to create the brain chemistry that will help us feel better. Conversely, if we eat mindlessly, we no doubt will contribute to the worsening of reward deficiency since its management is so reliant on proper nutrition.

## Self-Protective Behavior

What it all comes down to is, we are responsible for protecting ourselves from anything that threatens our sobriety, our stress levels, and our self-care. Learning to reduce stress where we can will afford us more control over self-care. New behaviors that can protect recovery can be learned. These behaviors can enable us to be firm in accepting our needs and not allowing other people or situations to push us into reactions that are not in our best interest.

To protect ourselves from unnecessary stress we must first identify our own stress triggers, those situations that might bring about an overreaction. We can then learn to change those situations, avoid them, reframe our perceptions and change our reactions, or learn how to interrupt them before they get too difficult to handle. This "take charge" behavior might mean leaving the room graciously when someone is chewing on an apple or crunching potato chips. Or it might mean asking someone not to smoke or being honest with people about our reactions to certain sounds. Remember, we can learn different behaviors for more control in situations where we have felt powerless in the past. Stress levels rise and fall depending upon the perception of how much control we have.

> Bea: *My son Brian has trouble with ADHD and when he's uncomfortable with the noise and frustration, he feels perfectly comfortable in getting up and walking out of a room. If he's at his girlfriend's house and the noise of the younger kids starts to get to him, he just takes a walk around the block. I didn't learn these protective behaviors until I was much older. I'm glad that Brian has learned them as young as he has.*

People with ADHD have a condition that demands as much "creative adaptability" as possible. Sometimes these creative steps may be as simple as taking a new, less noisy route to work, or eliminating several activities from a daily schedule that will slow the pace of living, or knowing some quiet retreat places to go once in a while for relaxation and clear thinking.

> Lee: *I think it's important to define what for me are safe places. Not just safe places but what is the safe amount of time for me to be somewhere. I need to feel free to say this is how long I will stay when I have to go somewhere or participate in some activity.*

Creative adaptability may mean finding adventuresome activity that does not overstimulate. Even people with overload need some excitement and adventure in their lives. We don't want to suggest that isolation and boredom are answers to the problem of overload.

We must take charge of our own recovery. We cannot wait around for the world to understand the symptoms of ADHD. It will not happen. We are the ones who must, as cooperatively as possible, let the world know. We must not hit people over the head with our disorder but simply take responsibility for it. We are the ones who have it. Having it is not our fault or anyone's fault. It just is. We simply must learn to live again in ways that protect our right to live as comfortably as possible.

## Keep It Simple

There is a phrase that can be heard throughout the halls of thousands of twelve-step groups held every day: "Keep it simple." Those of us who have ADHD have spent so much of life defending ourselves against it that many of us have made life more complicated than it needs to be.

Anne: *I have a horrible time with crowds and because of this I find the isolated beaches of Hawaii much more pleasant than the crowded ones of California. My stress levels are lower here and I can breathe better when people are farther away from me. Something that is good here is the simplicity of my surroundings. This quiets me. There is no loud music or loud talking. Keeping my surroundings simple is very important for me. When I lived with a roommate who had pictures all over everywhere, that really bothered me. I felt crowded and cramped by the pictures. I need to make open spaces for myself.*

Taking care of ourselves properly requires us to live more effectively. To do that we must learn to live more simply. This does not mean settling for mediocrity. But as we learn to think more clearly and feel better, we can learn to make more effective choices and cut down on the complexity in our lives. This is a full-time job! Not only are we simple people with complicated tastes, but the world is much more complex. There are many, many more decisions required of us than there were twenty years ago. Just trying to determine which breakfast cereal to buy can cause hyperventilation—unless we learn to keep it simple!

## Time-Out

There is great physiological and spiritual renewal in learning how to "step out" of our routine periodically and free ourselves of tyrannical expectations: expectations from work, expectations from a spouse, from kids, from relatives, from society. There are certainly benefits in fitting into a routine and being attached to family and friends. It's difficult to survive without others. But we also need to breathe once in a while and break free of those attachments. This can be for a few minutes, a few hours, or a few days.

Nancy: *I find it necessary to go "browsing" once a week. I take about four hours to do whatever I please. I may have a loose agenda or no agenda at all. I just attempt to do, in a healthy way, things I feel most like doing. At the end of this time-out I am usually much more refreshed to take on my regular routine and all that goes with it.*

The time-out activities should in some way be constructive, not just escapist. Often, if we use escape activities like eating and movie bingeing, we feel worse about ourselves than when we started. Positive alternatives range from playing tennis to going to a movie, from taking a nap to going on a ski trip, from going out to eat at the corner café to flying to Paris for dinner, from singing in the shower to going to the symphony.

Anne: *Another important part of my ADD management is journaling. I keep records of what's going on and try to pull my day together either in the morning as an exercise of planning or at night as an exercise of review. When I journal, it gives my life some framework. It narrows my thoughts down to what is specifically going on. I journal events and feelings. And sometimes just the different stuff going on in my head when it's spinning. When I do this, I can actually feel my thought processes slowing down. I can feel that change take place as I journal.*

Find ways to be creative, whether through writing, painting, photography, cooking. Whatever you do, and however long you do it, enjoy it as much as you can. During our ongoing journey of self-care, what is most critical to its success has to do with how well we are making friends with the present.

## Fun and Laughter

We cannot feel badly about ourselves or the world if we are laughing and having fun. People who struggle with ADHD usually have that wonderful capacity, despite the drudgery of the symptoms, to laugh at themselves and the world. It is a matter of survival to learn to do so. There is nothing more stimulating to the production of new reward brain chemistry than laughter, fun, and play. A deep belly laugh provides an endorphin lift that lasts for forty-five minutes. Most of us have had to work pretty hard at getting along in life. In self-care it's also important to play hard and laugh hard.

The stress, anger, and negativity that occur over and over again in the lives of those with ADHD take a great toll on the nervous system and inhibit the body's natural healing capability. Play and fun are relaxing, healing, stimulating, and freeing. After we laugh, we feel better, think better, and function better.

Learning to enjoy life means learning to live in the present—instead of regretting the past or waiting for the future. It is difficult for someone with ADHD to focus on the present, but when we can, we enjoy a richness to life that passes us by when we are always rushing to the next thing. Children have a lot to teach us about living in and enjoying the moment.

### At Play
by David

Come, child, blend with me.
The time is now,
as only time can be.
Come, child, let me share your world
where pain is a stranger,
and glances laced with sweet innocence,
dance on a world made just for you.

Come, child, let me into your eyes.
Share your world where time has no back or front,
just a middle where all is *now*
as you contemplate some beauty of nature

cast in this plant or that bug.
Come, child, I will honor this time
where we may touch this *now* together,
as I learn of your wisdom
that I passed so blindly by on the path to "adult."

Come, child, allow me into your joyful laughter—
that clean innocent music where love and joy were born.
Come, child, remind me through your dancing eyes
of when I, too, was eternal and praised the world
through uncluttered observations, never mindful or
caring of expectations the world was casting my way,
dulling my senses through its call to sameness,
where wrong is to be different, where it's wrong to be me.

Come, child, teach me your ways once again
and allow me into your space to rest,
to find forgotten fragments of my self,
to reacquaint myself with the magic moment,
to be all that I can be—here and *now*.

# 11

## Life Is More Than Just Surviving

Once upon a time, the animals decided they should do something meaningful to meet the problems of the new world. So they organized a school. They adopted an activity curriculum of running, climbing, swimming, and flying. To make it easier to administer the curriculum, all the animals took all the subjects.

The duck was excellent in swimming; in fact, better than his instructor. But he made only passing grades in flying, and was very poor in running. Since he was slow in running, he had to drop swimming and stay after school to practice running. This caused his web feet to be badly worn, so that he was only average in swimming.

The rabbit started at the top of his class in running, but developed a nervous twitch in his leg muscles because of so much make-up work in swimming. The squirrel was excellent in climbing, but he encountered constant frustration in flying class because his teacher made him start from the ground up instead of from the treetop down. He developed "charlie horses" from overexertion, and so only got a C in climbing and a D in running.

The eagle was a problem child and was severely disciplined for being a non-conformist. In climbing classes he beat all the others to the top of the tree, but insisted on using his own way to get there.[1]

**A**ccepting ourselves as we are (with our limitations) allows full expression of our potential within our boundaries. When we stop trying to change what is not within our power to change, we can redirect our energy to what is within our control. When we recognize that we may not have the ability to run like a horse, we may discover that we have the potential to fly like an eagle. It takes courage to give up trying to meet the expectations that life has handed us in order to become what we were created to be. There is an old saying: "When life hands you a lemon, make lemonade." But you can't do that as long as you do not recognize or accept that you have a lemon. If everyone around you keeps telling you that your lemon is a banana and you believe that, you may spend your life unsuccessfully trying to make banana nut bread.

Because of the shame that we have associated with the symptoms of ADHD, most of us spend enormous amounts of energy trying to hide our defects from ourselves and others. This offers us some degree of safety, but at quite a price! Hiding (from ourselves and others) saps all our creative juices. Accepting the truth of the effects of ADHD can seem overwhelming but is in fact the road to true freedom.

"I am not a bad person who chooses to be this way" is a realization that brings relief but also has tremendous potential to bring up rage (it is not fair) and grief (even if it isn't our fault we still have to pay the price). *Rage and grief are part of the work that can heal what cannot be cured.*

While it is useless to try to weigh one person's suffering against another's, for individuals with ADHD there is a time when it is necessary to come to the understanding that everyone has burdens that need attention. It is not a disease issue anymore. Ideally, you know your special needs well and have found a way to accommodate them in a self-care lifestyle that allows you to set boundaries and negotiate with your friends and family to accommodate your needs.

None of this work is worth it if there is not a payoff down the road, something more than survival. There must be something joyful too. When we are focused on the problems of ADHD, they consume all our thoughts. And as we grow in the understanding of what is needed we can restore our life to balance and free up energy. Healing what we cannot cure is a process that promises a potential for joyful living.[2]

At first, living with this new lifestyle seems chaotic and disruptive. All our energy goes into accommodating the "needs of the gene." Learning good self-care habits and putting them into practice takes time and energy. But after a while these lifestyle changes become habit, a rhythm that can sink into the background of everyday life. Someone has expressed it like this:

> There once was a field of tall prairie grass with a great tree nearby. The tree and grass would discuss many things over the long summer days. Inevitably the discussion would turn to the wind. It blew constantly. The tree would brag about its ability to withstand the wind because its roots were as deep as it was tall. The grass would merely sing in the wind sighing for the deep roots and the tallness of the tree. One day there came a great storm and mighty winds. The tree was rigid and strong in the face of the wind, the grass was pliant and blown almost flat in the wind. After the storm the tree had many branches broken, but the grass was intact, in fact the wind had helped to spread the seeds of the grass to new ground.

We can be like the tree trying to withstand the storm by resisting the wind of truth, or, like the grass, we can learn the ways to use the wind of truth to enhance our creative abilities. We can search ourselves for the particular gifts we have—to find what we do very well, to see ourselves as rich, abundant sources of physical, mental, social, and spiritual opportunities and possibilities. Life becomes an adventure.

## Balance

All of us seek a place where there is balance, where the fullness of our lives energizes us. Balance implies attention to all the parts of our humanness: our need for play, our need for work, our need for struggle, our need for peace, our need for beauty, our need for danger, our need for receiving, and our need for giving. This balance provides the energy to meet each day with some anticipation. Balanced living includes attention to self and attention to others—a little sacrifice, a little selfishness.

When we are attentive to the needs of our bodies it frees up energy. When we feel good about ourselves it is easier to think about our attitudes and values and to eliminate shame, guilt, and anger. When we are psychologically healthy it is easier to do those things that keep our bodies well. When our relationships are healthy we have support for personal growth. Acceptance of our condition and our need to care for ourselves in special ways frees us for something more.

Balanced living means that we are something larger than our individual physical, social, mental, and spiritual parts. Each of these aspects of our lives must interact and become something more. We are more than our physical brains. We are a marvelous and mysterious physical and spiritual entity.

> Anne: *How I'm doing spiritually has a lot to do with my ADHD and how I'm doing with my ADHD has a lot to do with how I'm doing spiritually. If I'm centered and living in the way I think God wants me to live, my ADHD is more settled. The stress of conflictual living seems to make the ADHD worse.*
>
> *Finding a way to center myself is important in managing my ADHD. The spiritual sense of who I am and whether or not I'm okay is important. Kind of like when as alcoholics we find out we are not bad people.*
>
> *In a real sense there is something "wrong" with me. My brain chemistry is different from other people's. I am different. But that is not a qualitative statement about me. It's not that I'm good or bad or right or wrong. I'm just different. That's important to me and it relates to being spiritually centered.*

## Living Creatively

Acceptance and balance become the means for reentering the world of relationship and creativity. As we are attentive to balance in our lives, the single most important skill is that of self-love. Forgiveness for not being able to be the "world's champion anything" is the source of growth. The bad days become part of the balancing process. Accepting our humanness is essential. From generosity to ourselves comes generosity toward others. Doing things we regret is part of the balance.

It is sometimes helpful to see ourselves in the way we see a baby. We are usually patient and generous with babies who are learning to sit up or crawl or walk. We see that they are learning and know that eventually they will catch on. Therefore, the screwups are merely ways that they learn. Each of us merely is trying to learn how to live. It is our definition of "the right way to live" that often gets us into trouble. Perfect is not a useful goal, making progress is. As we learn acceptance of our own particular way of experiencing the world, we begin to see ourselves as gifted instead of defective.

Joyful and creative living does not come from self-gratification—quick fixes to make us feel good, to cover up the pain. It comes from hard work, from looking at the world as it really is and finding ways to live creatively in that world, from comfort with who we are, and from the joy of discovering the unique truth that we are miraculously and wonderfully made.

Creative living calls us to live fully, with passion, to risk and play, to find the particular abilities we have and learn to express them. If there is nothing bright and new to move into, we can only long for what we have lost.

> Dawn: *I don't have ADHD. My friend Jeff does and sometimes he describes to me what he experiences. I am in awe. I feel like a blind, deaf person. I feel so inattentive to life. I know that being aware of every sight and sound in his environment is a burden for him much of the time. But when he is protected from overstimulation and chaos, he is so aware of beauty and abundance. He is so alive. He pays a price for this gift. But what a shame it would be if he couldn't find a way to express it. His ability to hear and to experience has become a rich resource and allowed him to become a gifted artist.*

Whether we are diabetic, arthritic, or have ADHD, we will only "recover" when we have found the capacity to live joyously and creatively with the *truth* of our health and when the needs of the physical body are honored and met. Through accepting the truth (living honestly) and striving for balance, we discover the meaning of a spiritual awakening, we become vitally aware of the presence of goodness. This allows us to love ourselves and to be generous toward others. To be awake spiritually is to be fully alive. A spiritual awakening is a personal experience that opens the door to meaningful and creative living.

There lives a creative being inside all of us and we must get out
of its way for it will give us no peace unless we do.
Mary Richards[3]

Creativity is so often limited by the boxes we put around the word
(confining it to art). But creativity is a source of energy. We are all creative artists! "Artist" is merely a word for those who try to express
what they have learned and how they see the world. In the process
of finding an earthworm, placing it on the clean kitchen counter, and
trying to tell his mom about it, a child becomes an artist. Creativity is
expressed in doing, thinking, playing, a statement of uniqueness as
beauty.

There is an interesting thing about the process of creativity. It is
often best utilized within limits. Limits create the frame for the work
to begin. You can only create a painting when you have defined the
edges of the canvas. This forces the artist to choose what to put in the
painting and what to leave out. The limitation becomes the resource
for the personal expression.

The limitations of ADHD can become a resource for personal creative expression. The paths we choose not to take in order to honor
the truth of our personal needs related to ADHD will send us down
paths that others will not take. Communication of what we see and
learn on this path becomes the resource for creative expression. The
more we follow and honor our own uniqueness and enhance it, the
more we need others and their diverse talents to complement our
own. Thus, creativity calls us to life with others, in balance with the
solitude of self that also fosters new creativity.

To live joyfully and creatively is not the same as perpetual happiness. Nothing creative is expressed without some struggle and pain.
Joyfulness is fullness of life, moving through the fear and pain rather
than avoiding it. Pain and suffering are a part of life. That's simply
the way it is. Each of us is born with special qualities that enable us to
see the world from a totally unique and new perspective. Many people die—seeking to escape struggle and pain—never discovering
what life holds for them in the way of opportunities and purposeful
living.

## Compassionate Living

Serendipity is the "happy accident" that often occurs while we are seeking something else. We start out looking for a particular thing and up pops something else. We compare what we are seeking with what pops up and decide the accidental discovery is better. Expecting the unexpected is to believe in a compassionate and cocreative universe.

As we begin to experience and believe in a compassionate, participating universe we find courage to go out on a limb, take some risks. We can let go of defensiveness and damage control as a way of living. Having looked squarely at our fears and weaknesses, we can be more open. We no longer need to fear that others will discover our weaknesses, the truth that we have spent our lives keeping anyone from knowing. We can extend to others an understanding of their fears and weaknesses. Out of acceptance of ourselves comes generosity toward others.

We have survived much personal agony, we are survivors of a way of experiencing the world that has cost us permanent damage to our self-image. The energy to come back from this devastation must be reinvested if we are to provide any meaning to the struggle. Pass it on. Pass on the lessons learned about the worth of every person, the mysterious gift that is diversity, the compassion and generosity to others who suffer.

Passing it on refills the cup of self-esteem and finally fills the hole someone else dug. We can only be healed when our personal journey through the hell of ADHD has been transformed into a resource for ourselves and others. It is the only way to transform a truly terrible loss into something useful.

The terrible truth is that you will never regain what you have lost. And most thinking and sensitive people would rather have back all they have lost. But since there was no choice in this matter, we are left with two options: accept the reality of what we have lost and learn to live well in spite of it or surrender to a deadly cesspool of diminished living—doomed to repeat over and over the attempt to make the truth not true. As for me, I choose Joy!

Anne Welch

Freedom is the result of allowing the truth to be true. We can choose life. We can commit to look for the possibilities where there are limits. We can choose to see people in the light of a universal struggle for something good. When we allow the truth to be true, blocks become a resource to our creativity and we lose our sense of helplessness. Courage is the only requirement, the courage to begin— with faith in the potential for an abundant and creative life.

# 12

## Hope for the Future

Forty years of research into the causes of substance use disorders and related behaviors have led to one conclusion: Irresistible craving is a malfunction of the reward centers of the brain involving the neurotransmitters and the enzymes that control them. Genetic research, including discovery of genetic links among these disorders, is just the beginning. Psychological and sociological research indicates that the environment can trigger, worsen, or to some degree alleviate the genetic predisposition, but the determining factors are biogenetic and biochemical. We are confident that the next few years will bring us much closer to cures for all forms of reward deficiency disorders, including ADHD.

We agree wholeheartedly with members of AA and other self-help groups and with most physicians and counselors that as yet there is no cure for addictive disorders. Abstinence is the only permanent solution for the alcoholic. But solutions to the problems of what we have called *reward deficiency syndrome* (RDS) may not be impossible dreams. Pharmacological intervention on behalf of the person with a substance use disorder is already a reality. Treatment adjuncts have been used to improve the general physical condition, ease the discomfort of withdrawal, and help the recovering patient remain sober. Genetic therapy holds out the possibility that someday we will be able to adjust genetic anomalies and break the genetic link that predisposes to ADHD, addiction, and other impulsive, compulsive disorders.

We now know that ADHD is a biogenetic condition that may be triggered by environmental factors. It seems certain that the search for the controlling genes may go forward in the decades ahead and probable that new discoveries will alter our approach to the prevention, diagnosis, and treatment. Indeed, we may be entering a new phase in "the decade of the brain" in the search for answers to the ancient questions: What causes mental diseases? How can they be prevented? How can they be identified early? How can they be cured?

In the past century, we have seen breakthroughs that have led to an understanding of bacteria and infections, to extraordinary progress of diagnostics and the art of surgery, and to a new understanding of the role of emotion in disease states. Now, we may be approaching the most exciting period in the history of the human sciences. We are watching the efforts of researchers as they push investigations in the fields of neurology, neuroscience, and addiction and behavioral disorders.

From earliest times, individuals and sometimes whole societies have self-medicated with substances found in the plant world—coca leaves, opium, and fermented sugars (alcohol)—to relieve their fears or discomforts or to replace a reward deficiency. We predict that someday in the future scientists will find new natural substances in the forests and in the oceans that will further enrich the pharmacological tools to potentially relieve the legacy of pain in the victims of reward deficiency.

We are watching the development of a new orientation toward the interaction of brain, emotion, and behavior that may affect us even more profoundly. As in the years when we watched psychosomatic medicine clarifying the roles of emotions in a variety of illnesses, we are beginning to understand that genetic defects leading to deficiencies and imbalances in neurotransmitters, enzymes, and receptors may give rise to a wide range of behavior disturbances.

Just as emotional and mental disturbances cause organic disturbances leading to physical illness, so cellular predisposition, deficiencies, or imbalances may cause not only emotional and mental disturbances such as addictive diseases but also anxiety, hostility, depression, reclusive or antisocial attitudes, conduct disorders, and antisocial personality disorder. These may not be primary aberrations, but may represent, instead, the effort of the mind to adapt to the consequences of defects in genes.

When we find the true genetic causes of neurochemical reward deficiency, we will begin to develop better diagnostic tools to make it possible to determine, for example, the degree of risk of the predisposition for substance use disorder in the prenatal period, in young children, in adults who may have the genetic predisposition (but may not have yet developed a substance use disorder), and in substance use disorder patients who enter treatment and want to know if their problem is genetic in origin. Since anxiety and anger and often violence may be manifestations of reward deficiency, it may be useful to explore the relationship between genetic neurotransmitter imbalances and exaggerated flight or fight responses.

Throughout this book we have taken up the challenge to establish addictive behaviors as an actual disease, not just a disease "concept," by showing that evidence supports the notion that vulnerability to addiction is genetically transmitted (especially in those individuals with problems severe enough to seek treatment). It is not necessary to establish that *all* addiction is caused by vulnerability. Heavy exposure to alcohol and drugs like cocaine and heroin or even nicotine and sugar may set in motion neurochemistry that may have similar end results as the underlying genetic anomalies.

For the person with ADHD who has entered the world of addictive behaviors and has overcome the dependence, the unfortunate and powerful dilemma that this individual must confront is the knowledge that without certain interventions, life is indeed a state of overload. So, the real culprit is not drugs, alcohol, carbohydrates, or sexual or gambling experience but the potential underlying biogenetic state. With this in mind, our primary goal should be to find a path that will break this legacy of pain. Not solely to help people with this condition attain a state of abstinence but to motivate their compulsive or impulsive nature in more productive and positive ways so that they and society can benefit from their genetic differences by utilizing their creativity, sensitivity, imagination, and sense of adventure.

This could be accomplished by early identification and implementation of physiological, psychological, and spiritual strategies. Right now there are few comprehensive resources available offering the kind of integrative services necessary to prevent or reduce the devastating consequences of ADHD and related behaviors. It is our hope for the future that more programs begin to integrate new and innovative modalities into their prevention and treatment approaches.

## Treatment

As we look into the future, we have a vision of specialized centers that would adapt the knowledge that we know exists in the fields of neurogenetics, neuroscience, neuropharmacology, psychotherapy, and spirituality to provide victims of impulsive, compulsive disorders with better diagnosis, more precise and targeted treatment, improved psychotherapy, and enhanced spiritual rebalancing.

Here is what we envision for Keith who is seeking help for a substance use disorder; he has used alcohol, marijuana, and cocaine to self-medicate reward deficiency symptoms. Although he has never been diagnosed with a specific disorder, he has had behavior, social, and learning problems all fourteen years of his life. His parents have brought him for help because of his substance use and escalating school problems.

At the center, Keith will be treated with dignity and respect, not as a person who *is* a problem but as a person who *has* a problem. He will be assessed, utilizing a number of diagnostic tools, to determine whether or not he has ADHD. Genetic testing will involve DNA tests for variance of at least three dopaminergic genes. Brain electrical activity mapping will be used particularly to determine the nature of Keith's P300 wave. Following a positive identification of ADHD (based on A1 allele presence in the dopaminergic system along with the typical ADHD profile) and positive history of substance use disorder, a team of specialists (including such professionals as a psychiatrist, a psychologist, a certified addictionologist, an addiction counselor, a neurologist, a neuropsychopharmacologist, a brain wave biofeedback therapist, and a nutritionist) will develop an individualized treatment plan for Keith. The modalities utilized in the center will be both traditional medical practices and alternative methods. Depending on the nature and severity of his problem, a number of procedures may be utilized in Keith's treatment.

First, Keith will be placed on a neuronutrient supplement to restore neurotransmitter imbalance in his brain. He will also be assessed to determine whether medication is likely to be beneficial for him and, if so, which medication is likely to help him most. Since Keith has an excess of theta brain waves (typical of people with ADHD), he will be trained to inhibit these waves by using brain wave biofeedback. Other techniques that have been demonstrated to be effective in improving the quality of life of an individual with ADHD will be utilized: cranial electrical stimulation, acupuncture, and treatments yet to be researched.

To ensure the most appropriate psychological care, Keith's treatment will focus on the shame and grief that accompany this disorder. As the above-mentioned therapies are helping Keith feel some relief from the symptoms of his disorder, he will have more strength to face some of his pain and work on the grief process. He will be allowed to acknowledge the losses of his life—the alienation from others, the missed opportunities, the never-to-be-recaptured experiences—feel the pain of those losses, and then move beyond them to focus on the gains.

He will become psychologically stronger as he learns the nature of his disorder and releases himself from any fault for having it. He will begin to see the strengths, control, and responsibility he has that will enable him to live productively in spite of it and even *because* of it. He will be enabled to move out of any sense of "victimization" into control and self-responsibility.

Spiritually, Keith will be encouraged into the process of sharing his pain, hope, and progress with others. He will be encouraged to find his own spiritual path. Through his participation in twelve-step meetings or other groups where he can be reconnected with himself, others, and the natural world, Keith will gain a renewed sense of companionship with a power outside of himself.

## Prevention

Through genetic testing we will be able to identify very early whether a child will be prone to a life of impulsive and addictive behaviors. Early identification will assist parents in understanding the potential despair and problems associated with ADHD. Teachers will be more prepared to deal with the child's behavior. Settings for learning will be modified to accommodate the child's symptoms. When children reach adolescence they will feel better about themselves because they haven't been put down; they will have had a more supportive environment; and they will have used brain chemistry rebalancing, brain wave regulation, and other approaches to enrich the environment of care that can lead to prevention of addiction.

## Hope for a Cure

As we enter the decade of the brain we are discovering astonishing things about the way the brain really works and about how our genetic makeup predicts, in part, how we behave. We have discussed that one gene in particular, the dopamine D2 receptor gene, is key in laying down the right number of receptors in the part of the brain termed the reward target site.

The dopaminergic genetic anomalies have been implicated in the reward deficiency syndrome, which includes aberrant behaviors from sex to drug cravings and even violent behaviors. We have argued that this provides great impetus to develop DNA tests to diagnose carriers of this genetic anomaly as a prevention tactic. We now suggest that sometime in the future scientists will develop ways to change the genetic state—such as flipping the A1 to the A2 form of the dopamine receptor gene—or will develop drugs to increase the number of D2 receptors. While the former technique involves gene manipulation and may take some time to achieve (even if we agree it is right to do this), the second possibility could be more immediate. A number of experimental compounds have already been shown to increase the dopamine D2 receptors quite specifically in animals.

While the use of genetic therapy as a potential "cure" for a neuro-chemical reward deficiency and/or ADHD seems simplistic and even scary, we find it quite compelling based on the new potential uses of gene therapy for central nervous system disorders (mental disorders). While our knowledge is still in an infancy state, the techniques have already been approved by government officials through the National Institutes of Health and have been accomplished for other diseases such as severe combined immunodeficiency disease (SCID) and cystic fibrosis and, most recently, for knocking out a brain tumor through a so-called suicide gene.

It is our strong belief that if we do not begin to accept at least the concept that our genes have something to do with our behavior and that genes may be equally as important as (or in some cases more important than) our environment and learned behavior, our nation's number one societal problem—drug addiction—will continue to wreak havoc in America.

This book is not about the pros and cons of genetic manipulation. Nor is it about the best mode of treatment for ADHD. It is instead about the biological basis of a behavioral response to uncontrollable elements that the ADHD person must confront every day. People that have this disease through genetic vulnerability should be elated to know that we are beginning to unravel the mystery of this disease, which was first identified over a century ago. Our vision of the future is a world where the chemical and electrical functions of the brain are understood; the problem of chemical imbalances as they affect behavior has been solved; the role of genetic anomalies in defective brain chemistry is understood; pharmaceutical and nutritional intervention as an adjunct to self-help programs is precise and effective; and the technique of defective gene therapy has been perfected, enabling us to break the genetic chain of inherited neurochemical reward deficiency disorders.

Envision a world where each individual will be able to enjoy the inborn legacy of reward and pleasure without having the need for addictive substances, without having to pay the price of addiction and pain. Just think how wonderful it would be if, because of this knowledge, victims of ADHD could become the beneficiaries of new approaches that could lead to a life free of overload.

❖
_____

# Afterword

Dear Fellow Traveler:

At this point, I want to speak to you, your true self, the one that has been covered up by fears, pain, masks, and the pretenses. It is my sincere hope that as we have shared our lives and work with you, you are beginning to see yourself differently and to see beyond your defenses and compensations to your true potential and gifts.

You cannot make up for lost time. You cannot undo the pain of the past. You *have* lived through painful circumstances and are probably still doing so, but you are surviving. We are survivors. And it is paradoxically through our survival that our best qualities, instincts, and sensitivities are culled.

We have spent our lives defending ourselves against life. We possess a sensitivity that can be invaded and overwhelmed by the world's cacophony. But because of our inborn uniqueness and because of what we have gained from our struggle, we have strength and beauty that can impact and change others and the world.

We are sensitive, soul-feeling people who not only hear the music but can hold hands with the notes, not only appreciate the sunset but commune with its beauty, touched to tears by reverence and awe. Our anger can be passion, our augmented perceptions can be delicate awareness, our drivenness can be energy to turn the world on its ear and make something bigger and better out of it. Our sensitive natures are not just to be defended but expanded and utilized to make the world a safer and more joyous place.

Because our sensitivity allows us to make connections with the earth and our environment, we are able to access a power of coequal relationships instead of a power gained out of domination and competition. Harmony with our world allows us an appreciation of the parts even when we can't see how they fit into the whole. We can appreciate the trees even when we can't find our way out of the forest.

Yes, relating so differently to a world wanting us to be the same can pin us against it and alienate us. We feel excluded from the norm. Not fitting in is always painful and yet it also offers a unique vantage point from which to see the world. It allows for our stories to be different. It allows us to see the world from a wonderfully unique and refreshing vantage point. Because of the bouncing, crooked, misfiring of neurons, we are able to see, feel, sense, and "be" in unique relationship to others and the world.

Pain and suffering have taken their toll on our bodies and minds. But these painful journeys have also imbued us with a perception that can offer strength and light that emerges from its darkness. Out of the very symptoms that skew our perception and make for a confusing world can come beauty, excitement, adventure, creativity, and fun. An ADHD miracle can shine forth out of the ashes of the destruction it has wrought. We can glean from it both pain and joy. We can embrace laughter as it rings across a sometimes dull reality and be thankful for our part in putting a little joy back in the world. Lord knows we need it.

We must first accept this character as our own and eventually learn to embrace it and love it. We must love ourselves in order to give ourselves and others the best of us. To know our gifts we must also know and accept our grief. Any way you cut it, there have been mountains of losses that have accumulated in our lives. These losses have been painful, sorrowful, and, in many cases, life-threatening.

To use our strengths we must touch our losses, mourn them, let go of them and allow them to work for us. We are—in this instant, right where we are—blessed with a character, passion, and compassion that others may not experience or understand. Some of us are blessed with an extraordinary sense of adventure, some of us with zany wit and rich laughter, some with artist souls and unusual creative perceptions, some with warm hearts and nurturing gifts, and many with sharp minds that always seem to be a step ahead of reality.

In order to do what you want to do, and even to put yourself in a position to know what that means, you must begin with acceptance of yourself. Right here, right now in this fragment of time, you must accept you as you are. In order to join the world, that same world that has so often rejected you, you must first move from the fear of isolation and retreat into an interaction with others. You must be willing to do more than learn to walk comfortably with that rock in your shoe. You must be willing to take it out and share your stuff with the world.

You can learn to confront that part of you that wants to just make it and plod along in mediocrity in order to avoid the pain. You can learn to embrace that adventurer in you that desires to fully express its uniqueness, that wants to shine. Embrace that shining spontaneity that is life itself. There are so many walking dead in the world, those people who have shut down and have come to passively endure life as a spectator rather than as a doer or interactant. Your spirit will not let that happen. It will not let you retreat for long without stirring your heart to come out and be. Follow that spirit and become all you can.

David Miller

### The Person Within

by David

Through jagged senses, nerves strung thin,
Remember that person, that spirit within;
The one holding tight as the gray winds blow;
The one holding fast way down below,
Under those layers shaped by the years
Of trials and tears,
By hopes and fears no one could see,
By dreams lost—never to be.

But given the power for what is to come,
He shines through the ashes and makes his run,
Dancing through darkness, up through the night,
Raging to the surface, shaped by the fight.
Ascending on song, on beauty's wing,
On nature's path I feel him spring,
Just as the river flows to the sea,
Rushing, reaching, rescuing me.
Up through the layers, shining through doubt
That has kept him away and me without
All the blessings that now can be
As we merge as one—this deep spirit and me.

# Appendix A
## Epilogue by Kenneth Blum, Ph.D.
## The Disease Precept: A View to the Future

Recently, I. Maltzman[1] reviewed the controversy of whether alcoholism is a disease or not by summarizing empirical research in the biopsychosocial field. While Maltzman carefully makes an important case for the assertion that alcoholism is a disease with both biogenic and psychosocial correlates, his primary focus is on the behavioral rather than the biogenic and physiological aspects of the disease. His arguments against controlled drinking and proponents of it[2] are well taken and have previously been discussed by me in *Alcohol and the Addictive Brain*.

Certainly, the report of long-term follow-up by Miller and associates was quite pessimistic and would argue against controlled drinking. Maltzman's review supports the disease concept of alcoholism and extends this view by providing some evidence to support the notion that the alcoholism syndrome is a consequence of brain dysfunction. I decided to further extend E.M. Jellinek's *(The Disease Concept of Alcoholism)* view by suggesting elsewhere the existence of a disease *precept* of alcoholism and other substance use disorders[3] by providing a plethora of scientific evidence primarily from the neuropharmacological literature.

The disease which we refer to as reward deficiency syndrome has multifactorial etiologies—probably polygenic in its origin—and therefore should be treated as a disease involving biogenic as well as psychogenic modalities for its prevention, diagnosis, and treatment. We believe that this concept supports the view of a psychoneurogenetic basis of addictive behavior as disease, or as J.R. Milam suggests, "a disease with a biogenic paradigm."[4]

While the psychogenic model is based on the nearly universal belief that alcoholism and other drug dependencies are symptoms or consequences of an underlying character defect, a destructive response to psychological and social problems, a learned behavior, Milam suggests that the biogenic model recognizes that alcoholism and substance use disorder is primarily an addictive response to the various drugs ingested in a *biologically susceptible* subject regardless of character and personality.

We emphasize the psychoneurogenic aspects supportive of the disease precept of not only addictive and compulsive behavior but, more important, ADHD and other related childhood behavior disorders that together have a common biogenic anomaly that we have called the reward deficiency syndrome. This precept idea is a modification of Milam's "biogenic paradigms" but essentially supports its view.

We also suggest that the genetic difference that causes people to be vulnerable may not be maladaptive under all circumstances. In medicine, there are examples where genetically transmitted differences have their advantages. Sickle cell anemia is a physiology that qualifies as a disease. Sickle cell traits, on the other hand, make people less likely to die from malaria which gives them a survival advantage in areas where malaria is common. We don't know whether the genetic vulnerability to addiction proffers any advantages. What is certain is that the physiology of some people is different. The different physiology is inherited and some similar changes can be induced by exposure to psychoactive chemicals.

Given all of this, it is our contention that even after prolonged abstinence from psychoactive drugs, craving remains but could take on other dimensions both positive (compulsive work) and negative (compulsive sex). It has been stated that genetic diseases seem an evolutionary blunder, an unjust fate decreed from the moment of conception. Yet they may be our protection against hidden dangers.

During the 1970s, research focus shifted from attempting to understand the physiological effects of drugs like alcohol to the mechanisms underlying craving behavior. Out of an enormous and growing accumulation of data there began to emerge a new understanding of the role of neurotransmitters and receptors and the enzymes that regulate their synthesis and breakdown. We began to see that the availability and balance and the action at receptors are keys to reward: pleasure, feelings of well-being, and euphoria.

The next step was the understanding that there is a blueprint that controls these neurochemical changes and interactions within the brain and that this blueprint is laid down by the genes. We now see growing evidence that any alteration or change is important in the neurochemistry of reward and may lead to compulsive, impulsive, and addictive disorders that I have termed the *reward deficiency syndrome*.

# Appendix B
# A Search for a Gene Associated with Alcoholism

## by Kenneth Blum, Ph.D.

The research tool used in my laboratory to identify a gene associated with alcoholism was a technique with the tongue-twisting name of Restriction Fragment Length Polymorphism (RFLP). To understand how this tool is used to study specific genes, it is necessary to understand the structure of DNA, which acts as a blueprint for manufacturing chemical products in the cell. Visualize the DNA as a twisted ladder with each side rail a DNA strand and each rung a pair of chemical bases. There are four of these bases: adenine (A), guanine (G), cytosine (C), and thymine (T). Each base can pair with only one other. That is, G *always* pairs with C, and T *always* pairs with A.

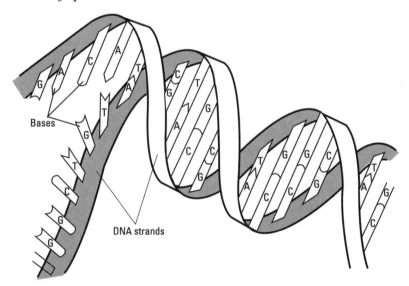

Figure 6. Structure of DNA. Simplified schematic of DNA, the structure of heredity. DNA is a twisted ladder, each side rail a DNA strand, and each rung a pair of chemical bases. Each of the four bases—adenine, guanine, cytosine, and thymine—can pair with only one of the other bases, that is, G with C, and T with A.

"Restriction enzymes" are special enzymes that researchers can use to snip out the exact gene they want from a long gene sequence. "Probes" are short lengths of DNA, obtained from another source, that will bind to a specific gene and only to that gene. In the research process, the DNA is placed in a solution and then cut into fragments by the restriction enzyme. A probe that has been made radioactive is added. If it matches the original DNA fragment, it binds to it and, because it is radioactive, shows up on a photographic film.

To use the RFLP technique effectively in my and Ernest Noble's search, three things were needed. The first was a road map of DNA that would help us locate where to look. The second was a source of DNA specimens from known alcoholics. The third was a source of gene probes that would bind to suspected sites on the target DNA.

The cascade theory provided the road map, narrowing the search down to genes involved in the manufacture of brain messengers (such as enkephalins, serotonin, GABA, and dopamine) that affected the reward area, and were already known to be associated with alcoholism. Brain samples supplied by Noble provided the source of DNA from people who had died from severe alcoholism and from a control sample of nonalcoholic brains. As for probes, queries around the world turned up over fifty candidate gene probes known to be involved in various aspects of alcoholism.

Noble had complete documentation on the brains in both samples, but since this was a "blind" experiment, scientists in my laboratory had no access to this information. We did not know whether a given DNA sample was from an alcoholic or a nonalcoholic brain.

What we were looking for was a difference in gene patterns that could be associated with alcoholism. As we accumulated pictures of various samples, they looked for one of three possibilities: patterns that were all the same; patterns that were different but not linked to a probe associated with the alcoholics or nonalcoholics in the study; or patterns that were different *and* linked to the alcoholics or nonalcoholics in the study.

After a year of frustrating failures where we investigated eight different gene probes (for example, one was associated with the breakdown of enkephalin and another associated with the production of an enzyme involved in the breakdown of alcohol), we finally tried a new probe that was associated with the dopamine D2 receptor gene. There are two variants of the dopamine D2 gene, called the "A1 allele" and the "A2 allele." After testing DNA from both alcoholics and nonalcoholics, we found that:

—80 percent of the nonalcoholics *did not* have the A1 allele
—69 percent of the alcoholics *did have* the A1 allele.

# Appendix C
## Attention Deficit Hyperactivity Disorder
## Genetic Studies

Early speculation about the causes of attention deficit hyperactivity disorder (ADHD) focused on such factors as marital disorder, poor parenting, brain damage, psychiatric illness, and being raised by alcoholic parents. But recent research gives evidence supporting the role of genetics in ADHD.

A number of studies have shown that fathers and/or mothers of ADHD children tend to have antisocial personality and alcoholism.[1] Numerous studies have indicated that 20 to 30 percent of siblings of ADHD children also have ADHD.[2]

Other studies showed that 22 percent of brothers and 8 percent of sisters of hyperactive children were hyperactive themselves. Interestingly, however, when attention deficit was considered without hyperactivity, the number of brothers and sisters affected was equal. This could explain why boys are more likely to be identified as having attention deficit hyperactivity disorder with hyperactivity while girls are identified as having attention deficit without hyperactivity.[3]

In one study of ADHD children it was found that if neither parent had the syndrome, 11 percent of the siblings had it. If one parent had ADHD, 34 percent of the siblings had it.[4] The fact that parents with ADHD have a child with it does not prove that the problem is genetic. The question can be asked. "Was the behavior learned?"

One answer to the question is to look at siblings and halfsiblings, both raised in the same environment. If ADHD is learned, the frequency should be the same for both. In actuality, halfsiblings who have only half the genetic similarity show a significantly decreased frequency of ADHD.

In one study of twins, if one identical twin had ADHD, the other also had ADHD. If a fraternal twin had ADHD, only 17 percent of the other twins had ADHD.[5] This finding was confirmed in two other independent studies.

Another approach is to look at the parents of ADHD children given up for adoption. If ADHD is a genetic disorder, the biological parents of children with the problem should show a higher frequency of ADHD. In a study of ADHD children born to ADHD parents but adopted at birth, the rate of antisocial personality and alcoholism, as well as the rate of ADHD, were higher in biological parents than adoptive parents.[6]

Numerous studies have found a significant correlation between ADHD and adult substance use disorders. These findings suggest that childhood behavioral disorders may signal a genetic predisposition to addiction.

# Appendix D
## Assessment Questionnaire[1]

If you are recovering from an addiction and are wondering if you may have attention deficit hyperactivity disorder, the following questionnaire may help you figure out if you need to get a professional diagnosis and treatment.

### Symptoms of Stimulus Augmentation

As a child or teenager, before you started drinking or using other drugs, did you *frequently*

1. become distracted easily by sights and sounds such as traffic outside, blinking lights, people talking nearby, or a radio playing in another room? ___yes ___no
2. feel overwhelmed or bombarded by these above-mentioned environmental sights or sounds? ___yes ___no
3. feel that these distractions interfered with your ability to focus or concentrate on a specific task? ___yes ___no
4. feel highly stressed or anxious when experiencing this sense of distraction?___yes ___no

### Symptoms of Inattention

As a child or teenager, before you started drinking or using other drugs, did you *frequently*

1. fail to complete tasks or to follow through on instructions from others?___yes ___no
2. have difficulty paying attention during activities where you were expected to do so for a long time? ___yes ___no
3. have difficulty organizing tasks or activities or trouble maintaining an organized living place? ___yes ___no
4. lose things necessary for performing tasks? ___yes ___no
5. forget things important to your daily activity? ___yes ___no
6. have difficulty paying attention to details? ___yes ___no

7. avoid or dislike tasks that require mental effort for a substantial period of time? ___yes ___no
8. have trouble remembering to do a task or remembering what someone told you? ___yes ___no
9. have difficulty solving what may seem like simple problems to others? ___yes ___no
10. have difficulty concentrating even when it seems important to do so? ___yes ___no
11. find yourself easily distracted? ___yes ___no
12. feel that things are jumbled or chaotic when to others they seem orderly? ___yes ___no
13. start one thing before you finish something else? ___yes ___no
14. have a tendency to daydream or get called a daydreamer ___yes ___no
15. find it difficult to stay motivated to accomplish a goal? ___yes ___no
16. put things off until it was impossible to get them done? ___yes ___no
17. get good ideas and then never follow through on them? ___yes ___no

## Symptoms of Hyperactivity or Impulsivity

As a child or teenager, before you started drinking or using other drugs, did you *frequently*

1. have an ongoing sense of being in a hurry or feel a need to always be on the go? ___yes ___no
2. have difficulty remaining seated when expected to do so? ___yes ___no
3. have difficulty waiting your turn or waiting in line? ___yes ___no
4. blurt out answers before questions have been completed? ___yes ___no
5. interrupt the conversations of others or intrude on activities of others? ___yes ___no
6. hear from others that you talk too much?___yes ___no
7. have people tell you that you don't listen? ___yes ___no
8. move excessively or often feel impatient or restless? ___yes ___no

9. fidget, squirm, drum your fingers, tap your feet, or pace?
___yes ___no
10. have difficulty engaging in quiet activities with others?
___yes ___no
11. seem to be accident-prone? ___yes ___no
12. engage in dangerous activities without considering the consequences? ___yes ___no
13. make impulsive decisions without fully considering the consequences? ___yes ___no

## Consequences of Symptoms of ADHD

As a child or teenager, before you started drinking or using other drugs, did you *frequently*

1. overreact to what you were feeling so that later you wondered why you acted that way? ___yes ___no
2. feel overly anxious? ___yes ___no
3. feel emotionally numb? ___yes ___no
4. have difficulty maintaining friendships or close relationships? ___yes ___no
5. have anger outbursts related to low frustration tolerance? ___yes ___no
6. hear from others that you could do much better if you would just try harder (when you were trying as hard as you knew how?) ___yes ___no
7. have a low opinion of yourself? ___yes ___no
8. feel overwhelmed by the tasks of daily living? ___yes ___no
9. get lost easily? ___yes ___no
10. need structure and routine but find it impossible to create it? ___yes ___no
11. have inconsistent school performance? ___yes ___no
12. have frequent traffic violations? ___yes ___no
13. seek out stimulating or exciting activities? ___yes ___no
14. look for quiet places to be alone? ___yes ___no

## Appendix D

### Symptoms While Abstinent

If you answered only a few of the preceding questions yes, you probably do not have attention deficit hyperactivity disorder. Everyone experiences some of these things at times. If you answered more than just a few of these questions yes, answer the following questions about how these symptoms were affected by your drinking or drug use. While drinking or using drugs did you usually

1. feel more in control of your thoughts? ___yes ___no
2. feel more in control of your feelings? ___yes ___no
3. feel less distracted by sights and sounds around you? ___yes ___no
4. feel that drinking/using improved your ability to remember? ___yes ___no
5. feel better able to pay attention? ___yes ___no
6. feel less stressed by noise and sights going on around you? ___yes ___no
7. feel that drinking/using improved your ability to do certain tasks? ___yes ___no

If you answered yes to most of these questions you were probably finding relief from ADHD symptoms by drinking or using other drugs. Did these symptoms return when you stopped drinking/using? If so, you should see someone qualified to make an accurate diagnosis for ADHD.

# Notes

## Introduction by David Miller

1. Gordon E. Barnes, "The Alcoholic Personality: A Reanalysis of the Literature," *Journal of Studies on Alcohol*, vol. 40, no. 7 (1979).

2. Ralph E. Tarter and Kathleen Edwards, "Psychological Factors Associated with the Risk for Alcoholism," *Alcoholism: Clinical and Experimental Research*, vol. 12, no. 4 (July/August 1988).

3. David E. Comings, "The Genetics of Addictive Behaviors: The Role of Childhood Behavioral Disorders, *Addiction and Recovery* (November/December 1991).

4. A.I. Alterman and R.E. Tarter, "The Transmission of Psychological Vulnerability: Implications for Alcoholism Etiology," *Journal of Nervous Mental Disorders* 171 (1983): 147–154.; D.W. Goodwin, F. Schulsinger, L. Hermansen, S.B. Guze, and G. Winokur, "Alcoholism and the Hyperactive Child Syndrome," *Journal of Nervous Mental Disorders* (1975) 160: 349–353; R.E. Tarter, H. McBride, N. Buonpane, and D.U. Schneider, "Differentiation of Alcoholics: Childhood History of Minimal Brain Dysfunction, Family History, and Drinking Pattern," *Archives of General Psychiatry* 34 (1977): 761–768.

5. David E. Comings, "The Genetics of Addictive Behaviors: The Role of Childhood Behavioral Disorders," *Addiction and Recovery* (November/December 1991).

6. Ralph E. Tarter, Andrea M. Hegedus, Gerald Goldstein, Carolyn Shelly, and Arthur I. Alterman, "Adolescent Sons of Alcoholics: Neuropsychological and Personality Characteristics," *Alcoholism: Clinical and Experimental Research*, vol. 8, no. 2 (March/April 1984).

7. C. Ryan and B. Butters, "Learning and Memory Impairments in Young and Old Alcoholics: Evidence for the Premature-Aging Hypothesis," *Alcoholism* 4 (1980): 288–293.

8. B. Jones and O. Parsons, "Impaired Abstracting Ability in Chronic Alcoholics," *Archives of General Psychiatry* 24 (1971): 71–75; R. Tarter, "An Analysis of Cognitive Deficits in Chronic Alcoholics," *Journal of Nervous Mental Disorders* 157 (1973): 138–174; O. Parsons, "The Neuropsychology of Alcohol and Drug Abuse," in *Handbook of Clinical Neuropsychology*, eds. S. Filskov and T. Boll (New York: John Wiley & Sons, 1981).

9. Ralph E. Tarter, Andrea M. Hegedus, Gerald Goldstein, Carolyn Shelly, and Arthur I. Alterman, "Adolescent Sons of Alcoholics: Neuropsychological and Personality Characteristics," *Alcoholism: Clinical and Experimental Research*, vol. 8, no. 2 (March/April 1984).

10. J. Morrison and M. Steward, "The Psychiatric Status of the Legal Families of Adopted Hyperactive Children," *Archives of General Psychiatry* 28 (1973): 888–891; Ralph E. Tarter, Ph.D., Andrea M. Hegedus, M.P.A., and Joan S. Gavaler, B.S., "Hyperactivity in Sons of Alcoholics," *Journal of Studies on Alcohol,* vol. 46, no. 3 (1985).

11. Ralph E. Tarter and Kathleen Edwards, "Psychological Factors Associated with the Risk for Alcoholism," *Alcoholism: Clinical and Experimental Research*, vol. 12, no. 4 (July/August 1988); J. Biederman, K. Munir, D. Knee, W. Habelow, M. Armentano, S. Autor, S.K. Hoge, and C. Waternaux, "A Family of Patients with Attention Deficit Disorder and Normal Controls," *Journal of Psychiatry Research* 20 (1986): 263–274; R. Schachar and R. Wachsmuth, "Hyperactivity and Parental Psychopathology," *Journal of Child Psychological Psychiatry* 31 (1990): 381–392.

12. Ralph E. Tarter and Kathleen Edwards "Psychological Factors Associated with the Risk for Alcoholism," *Alcoholism: Clinical and Experimental Research,* vol. 12, no. 4 (July/August 1988); L. Hennecke, "Stimulus Augmenting and Field Dependence in Children of Alcoholic Fathers," *Journal of Studies on Alcohol* 45 (1984): 486–492.

13. Ralph E. Tarter and Kathleen Edwards, "Psychological Factors Associated with the Risk for Alcoholism," *Alcoholism: Clinical and Experimental Research*, vol. 12, no. 4 (July/August 1988).

14. D. Wood, P. Wender, and F.W. Reimherr, "The Prevalence of Attention Deficit Disorder, Residual Type, or Minimal Brain Dysfunction in a Population of Male Alcoholic Patients," *American Journal of Psychiatry* 140 (1983): 95–98.

15. D.W. Goodwin, "Alcoholism and Heredity," *Archives of General Psychiatry* 36 (1979): 57–61.

16. L. Hennecke, "Stimulus Augmenting and Field Dependence in Children of Alcoholic Fathers," *Journal of Studies on Alcohol* 45 (1984): 486–492.

17. L. Hennecke, "Stimulus Augmenting and Field Dependence in Children of Alcoholic Fathers, *Journal of Studies on Alcohol* 45 (1984): 486–492.

### Introduction: The Scientific Viewpoint by Kenneth Blum, Ph.D.

1. K. Blum, P.J. Sheridan, R.C. Wood, E.R. Braverman, T.J.H Chen, and D.E. Comings, "Dopamine D2 receptor gene variants: association and linkage studies in impulsive-addictive-compulsive behavior," *Pharmacogenetics* 5 (1995): 121–141.

### Chapter 2

1. D.E. Comings, *Tourette Syndrome and Human Behavior* (Duarte, California: Hope Press, 1995).

2. *Diagnostic and Statistical Manual of Mental Disorders, Fourth Edition* (Washington D.C., American Psychiatric Association, 1995).

3. Ibid.

4. Ibid.
5. Ibid.
6. Ibid.
7. Ibid.
8. Ibid.

## Chapter 3

1. In 1994, Jay M. Giedd, M.D., and associates, by means of quantitative neuroanatomic imaging in eighteen boys with ADHD and eighteen carefully matched normal boys, supported the theory of abnormal frontal lobe development and function in ADHD.

2. Joel F. Lubar, "Discourse on the Development of EEG Diagnostics and Biofeedback for Attention-Deficit/Hyperactivity Disorders," *Biofeedback and Self-Regulation*, vol. 16, no. 3 (1991).

3. A.J. August and M.A. Stewart, "Familial subtypes of childhood hyperactivity," *Journal of Nervous and Mentory Diseases* 171 (1983): 362–368.

4. A.J. August, M.A. Steward, and C.S. Holmes, "A four-year follow-up of hyperactive boys with and without conduct disorder," *British Journal of Psychiatry* 143 (1983): 192–198.

5. S.V. Faraone, J. Biederman, K. Keenman, T.M. Tsuang, "Separation of DSM-III attention deficit disorder and conduct disorder: evidence from a family-genetic study of american child psychiatric patients," *Psychological Medicine* 21 (1991): 109–121; J. Biederman, K. Munir, D. Knee, W. Habelow, M. Armentano, S. Autor, S.K. Hoge, and C. Waternaux, "A Family of Patients with Attention Deficit Disorder and Normal Controls," *Journal of Psychiatry Research* 20 (1986): 263–274.

6. David E. Comings, M.D., "The Genetics of Addictive Behaviors: The Role of Childhood Behavioral Disorders," *Addiction and Recovery* (November/December 1991).

## Chapter 4

1. K. Blum, E.P. Noble, P.J. Sheridan, A. Montgomery, T. Ritchie, P. Jagadeeswaran, H. Nogami, A.H. Briggs and J.B. Cohn, "Allelic association of human dopamine D2 receptor gene in alcoholism," *Journal of the American Medical Association* 263 (1990): 2055–2060.

## Chapter 5

1. Eric J. Simon (New York University Medical Center), Avram Goldstein (Stanford University in California), Lars Terenius (University of Upsala in Sweden) in 1971; Candace Pert and Sol Snyder (Johns Hopkins University School of

Medicine in Baltimore). E.J Simon, "Opiate receptors: isolation and mechanisms," in K. Blum, ed., *Alcohol and opiates, Neurochemistry and Behavioral Mechanisms* (New York: Academic Press, 1977), 253–264.

2. Hans Kosterlitz and John Hughes in Aberdeen, Lars Terenius and Agneta Wahlstom in Sweden, Solomon Snyder in Baltimore, Nobel Prize–winner Roger Guillemin in California, and Avram Goldstein in California, using a special technique that enabled them to visualize enkephalins in the brain, realized that these substances, like neurotransmitters, were highly concentrated on the membranes of nerve endings. G. Terenius, "Stereospecific interaction between narcotic analgesics and symantic plasma membrane fraction of rat cerebral cortex," *Acta Pharmacologica and Toxicologica* 32 (1973): 317–320.

3. J. Hughes, T.W. Smith, H.W. Kosterlitz, L.A. Fathergill, B.A. Morgan, H.R. Morris, "Identification of two related pentapeptides from the brain with patient opiate agonist activity, *Nature* 258 (1975): 77–80.

4. The other researchers made similar discoveries, identifying MLF (morphine-like factor, MLS (morphinelike substances), POP (pituitary opioid peptide), and endorphins (a term coined by Eric Simon meaning "endogenous morphine"). L.H. Lazarus, W. Ling, and R. Guillemin, "Beta-Lipoprotein as a prohormone for the morphoromimetic peptides, endorphins and enkephalins," *Proceeding of the National Academy of Science* 73 (1976): 2156–5; B.M. Cox, A. Goldstein, C.H. Li, "Opioid activity of a peptide with opiate activity from camel pituitary glands," *Proceeding of the National Academy of Science* 73 (1976): 1821–1823; C.B. Pert and S.H. Snyder, "Opiate receptor: demonstration in nervous tissue," *Science* 1731 (1973): 1011–1014.

5. M. A. Korsten, S. Matsuzaki, A. Feinman, and C.S. Lieber, "High Blood Acetaldehyde Levels after Ethanol Administration: Difference between Alcoholic and Non-alcoholic Subjects," *New England Journal of Medicine* 292 (1975): 386–389.

6. M.A. Schuckit and V. Rayses, "Ethanol Ingestion: Differences in Blood Acetaldehyde Concentrations in Relatives of Alcoholics and Controls," *Science* 203 (1979): 54–55.

7. For example: Alcohol acts through TIQs to stimulate opiate receptors, inhibiting GABA and causing the release of dopamine at reward sites. Morphine acts directly to stimulate opiate receptors, inhibiting GABA and causing the release of dopamine at reward sites. Cocaine acts directly to release dopamine at the reward sites. Glucose acts indirectly by causing the release of opiate peptides which inhibit GABA and cause the release of dopamine at receptor sites. K. Blum, and James Payne, *Alcohol and the Addictive Brain* (New York: The Free Press, 1991).

## Chapter 7

1. One study by Norman Miller reported that 50 percent of drug abusers had at least one close relative with a diagnosis of alcohol dependence. Anothers found that 57 percent of fathers and 12 percent of brothers of opiate addicts were alcoholics.

2. M. A. Schuckit, D.W. Goodwin, and G. Winokur, "A Study of Alcoholism in Half-Siblings," *American Journal of Psychiatry* 128 (1972): 1132–1136; D.S. Goodwin, "Alcoholism and heredity, "*Archives of General Psychiatry* 36 (1979): 57–61; C.R. Cloninger, M. Bohman, and S. Sigvardsson, "Inheritance of Alcohol Abuse, *Archives of General Psychiatry* 38 (1983): 861–868.

3. H. Begleiter, B. Porjesz, and C.L. Chiu, "Auditory Brainstem Potentials in Chronic Alcoholics," *Science* 211 (1981): 1064–1066; C.R. Cloninger, M. Bohman, and S. Sigvardsson, "Inheritance of Alcohol Abuse," *Archives of General Psychiatry* 38 (1983): 861–868.

4. K. Blum, E.P. Noble, P.J. Sheridan, A. Montgomery, T. Ritchie, P. Jagadeeswaran, H. Nogami, A.H. Briggs, and J.B. Cohn, "Allelic association of human dopamine D2 receptor gene in alcoholism," *Journal of the American Medical Association* 263 (1990): 2055–2060.

5. K. Blum, E.R. Braverman, M.J. Dinardo, R.C. Wood, and P.J. Sheridan, "Prolonged P300 latency in a neuropsychiatric population with the D2 dopamine receptor A1 allele," *Pharmacogenetics* 4 (1994): 313–322.

6. E.P. Noble, K. Blum, H. Khalsa, T. Ritchie, A. Montgomery, R.C. Wood, R.J. Fitch, T. Ozkaragoz, P.J. Sheridan, M.D. Anglin, A. Paredes, L.J. Treiman, and R.S. Sparkes, "Allelic association of the D2 dopamine receptor gene with cocaine dependence," *Drug and Alcohol Dependence* 33 (1993): 271–285.

7. D.E. Comings, B.G. Comings, D. Muhleman, G. Dietz, B. Shahbahrami, D. Tast, E. Knell, K. Kocsis, R. Baumgarten, B.M. Kovacs, D.L. Levy, M. Smith, R.L. Borison, D.D. Evans, D.N. Klein, J. MacMurray, J.M. Tosk, J. Sverd, R. Gysin, and S.D. Flanagan, "The dopamine D2 receptor locus as a modifying gene in neuropsychiatric disorders," *Journal of the American Medical Association* 266 (1991): 1793–1800.

8. E.P. Noble, K. Blum, H. Khalsa, T. Ritchie, A. Montgomery, R.C. Wood, R.J. Fitch, T. Ozkaragoz, P.J. Sheridan, M.D. Anglin, A. Paredes, L.J. Treiman, and R.S. Sparkes, "Allelic association of the D2 dopamine receptor gene with cocaine dependence," *Drug and Alcohol Dependence* 33 (1993): 271–285.

9. G.R. Uhl, K. Blum, E.P. Noble, and S.S. Smith, "D2 receptor gene—the cause or consequence of substance abuse," *Trends in Neuroscience* 17 (1994): 50–51.

10. D.E. Comings, B.G. Comings, D. Muhleman, G. Dietz, B. Shahbahrami, D. Tast, E. Knell, K. Kocsis, R. Baumgarten, B.M. Kovacs, D.L. Levy, M. Smith, R.L. Borison, D.D. Evans, D.N. Klein, J. MacMurray, J.M. Tosk, J. Sverd, R. Gysin, and S.D. Flanagan, "The dopamine D2 receptor locus as a modifying gene in neuropsychiatric disorders," *Journal of the American Medical Association* 266 (1991): 1793–1800.

11. D.E. Comings, D. Muhleman, C. Ahn, R. Gysin, and S.D. Flanagan, "The D2 Gene, A Genetic Risk Factor in Substance Abuse," *Drugs and Alcohol Dependence* 34 (1994): 175–180.

12. Dennis Daley, ed., *Relapse: Conceptual, Research, and Clinical Perspective* (New York: The Haworth Press, 1989).

13. G.E. Swan, D. Cormelli, R.H. Rosenman, R.R. Fabsitz, J.C. Christian,

"Smoking and Alcohol Consumption in Adult Males Twins: Genetic Heritability and Shared Environmental Influences," *Journal of Substance Abuse* 2 (1990): 35–50.

14. Ibid.

15. E.P. Noble, S.T. St. Jeor, T. Ritchie, K. Syndulko, S.C. St. Jeor, R.J. Fitch, R.L. Brunner, and R.S. Sparkes, "D2 dopamine receptor gene and cigarette smoking: a reward gene?" *Medical Hypotheses* 42 (1994): 257–260.

16. D.E. Comings, L. Ferry, S. Bradshaw-Robinson, R. Burchette, C. Chiu, D. Muhleman, "The dopamine D2 receptor (DRD2) gene: a genetic risk factor in smoking," *Pharmacogenetics* (in press, 1995).

17. D.E. Comings, R.J. Rosenthal, H.R. Lesieur, L. Rugle, D. Muhleman, C. Chiu, G. Dietz, and R. Gade, "The molecular genetics of pathological gambling: the DRD2 gene" (submitted, 1995).

18. Ibid.

19. L. Eisenberg, "Psychiatric Implications on Brain Damage in Children," *Psychiatric Quarterly* 31 (1957): 72–92.

20. A.K. Shapiro and E.S. Shapiro, "Do stimulants provoke, cause or exacerbate tics and tourette syndrome?" *Compr. Psychiatry* 22 (1981): 265–273.

21. D.E. Comings, *Tourette Syndrome and Human Behavior* (Duarte, California: Hope Press, 1990), 641–648.

22. D.E. Comings, B.G. Comings, D. Muhleman, G. Dietz, B. Shahbahrami, D. Tast, E. Knell, K. Kocsis, R. Baumgarten, B.M. Kovacs, D.L. Levy, M. Smith, R.L. Borison, D.D. Evans, D.N. Klein, J. MacMurray, J.M. Tosk, J. Sverd, R. Gysin, and S.D. Flanagan, "The dopamine D2 receptor locus as a modifying gene in neuropsychiatric disorders," *Journal of the American Medical Association* 266 (1991): 1793–1800.

23. D.E. Comings, H. Wu, C. Chiu, R.H. Ring, G. Dietz, and D. Muhleman, "Polygenic inheritance of tourette syndrome, ADHD, conduct and oppositional definant disorder: the additive and subtractive effect of the DRD2, DßH, and DAT1 genes" (submitted 1995).

24. B. Hauser, J.A. Matochik, J. Miyson, and B.D Weintraub, "Attention Deficit-Hyperactivity Disorder in People with Generalized Resistance to Thyroid Hormone," *New England Journal of Medicine* 328(14) (1993): 997–1001.

25. D.E. Comings, *Tourette Syndrome and Human Behavior* (Duarte, California: Hope Press, 1990), 399–400.

26. Marc A. Schuckit, "Is There a Relationship Between Hyperactivity in Childhood and the Risk for Alcoholism?" *Drug Abuse and Alcoholism Newsletter,* vol. 24, no. 5 (October 1995).

27. Ibid.

28. D.E. Commings, *The Discovery of Tourette and Other Human Behavior Genes,* (Durarte, California: Hope Press, 1995).

29. Ibid.

## Chapter 8

1. J. Kagan, et al., "Information Processing in the Child: Significance of Analytic and Reflective Attitudes," *Psychological Monographs* 78 (1, No. 578).

2. L.M. Greenberg, *Test of Variables of Attention Computer Program Manual* (St. Paul, Minnesota: Attention Technology, 1990).

3. H. Begleiter, B. Porjesz, and C.L. Chiu, "Auditory Brainstem Potentials in Chronic Alcoholics," *Science* 211 (1981), 1064–1066; A. Pfefferbaum, T.B. Horvath, W.T. Roth, and B.S. Kopell, "Event related potential changes in chronic alcoholics," *Electroencephalogy Clin Neurophysiol,* 47 (1979): 637–47; A. Pfefferbaum, J.M. Ford, P.M. White, and D. Mathalon, "Event related potentials in alcoholic men: P3 amplitude reflects family history but not alcohol consumption," *Alcoholism: Clinical and Experimental Research* 15 (1991): 839–850; H. Begleiter, B. Porjesz, and M. Tenner, "Neuroradiological and Neurophysiological Evidence of Brain Deficits in Chronic Alcoholics," *Acta Psychiatrica Scandinavica* 62 (Suppl. 283) (1980): 3–13; B. Porjesz and H. Begleiter, "Visual Evoked Potentials and Brain Dysfunction in Chronic Alcoholism," in H. Begleiter, ed., *Evoked Brain Potentials and Behavior* (New York: Plenum, 1979), 277–302.

4. H. Begleiter and B. Porjesz, "Neurological processes in individuals at risk for alcoholism" *Alcohol and Alcoholism* 25 (2/3) (1990): 251–256; S. O'Connor, V. Hesselbrock, and A. Tasman, "Correlates of Increased Risk for Alcoholism in Young Men," *Progress Neuropsychopharmacology Biological Psychiatry* 10 (1986): 211–218; S. O'Connor, V. Hesselbrock, A. Tasman, and N. DePalma, "P3 Amplitudes in Two Distinct Tasks are Decreased in Young Men with a History of Paternal Alcoholism," *Alcohol* 4 (1987): 323–330; H. Begleiter, B. Porjesz, B. Bihari, and B. Kissin, "Event-related Brain Potentials in Boys at Risk for Alcoholism," *Science* 225 (1984): 1493–1496; H. Begleiter and B. Porjesz, "Potential biological markers in individuals at high risk for developing alcoholism: an atypical neurocognitive profile in alcoholic fathers and their sons," *Alcoholism: Clinical and Experimental Research* 4 (12) (1988): 488–493.

5. Kristin Swartz and Eric Braverman, M.D., "Cranial Electrotherapy Stimulation (CES)," *Townsend Letter for Doctors* (December 1991); E.R. Braverman, K. Blum, and R.J. Smayda, "A commentary on brain mapping in 60 substance abusers: can the potential for drug abuse be predicted and prevented by treatment?" *Current Therapeutic Research* 48(4) (1990): 569–585.

6. K. Blum, E.R. Braverman, M.J. Dinardo, R.C. Wood, and P.J. Sheridan, "Prolonged P300 latency in a neuropsychiatric population with the D2 dopamine receptor A1 allele," *Pharmacogenetics* 4 (1994): 313–322.

## Chapter 9

1. Hans R. Huessy, M.D., *"Attention Deficit Disorder: What Is It?,"* University of Vermont College of Medicine, Department of Psychiatry (unpublished, 1992).

2. Edward M. Hallowell and John J. Ratey, M.D., *Driven to Distraction* (New York: Pantheon Books, 1994), 237.

3. Edward M. Hallowell and John J. Ratey, M.D., *Driven to Distraction* (New York: Pantheon Books, 1994), 238.

4. C.T. Gualtieri, M.G. Ondrusek, and C. Finley, "Attention Deficit Disorders in Adults," *Clinical Neuropharmacology* 8 (1985): 343-356.

5. Michael Tranfaglia, M.D, "The Readers' Forum," *Challenge* (January/February 1995), 9.

6. Edward M. Hallowell and John J.,Ratey, M.D., *Driven to Distraction* (New York: Pantheon Books, 1994), 240-241.

7. Ibid.

8. Hans R. Huessy, M.D., "Attention Deficit Disorder: What Is It?," University of Vermont College of Medicine, Department of Psychiatry (unpublished, 1992).

9. Merlene Miller, Terence T. Gorski, and David Miller, *Learning To Live Again* (Independence, Missouri: Herald House/Independence Press, 1992), 305.

10. J.R. Volpicelli, A.I. Alterman, M. Hayashida, and C.P. O'Brien, "Naltrexone in the Treatment of Alcohol Dependence," *Archives of General Psychiatry,* vol. 49 (November 1992).

11. Joel F. Lubar, "Discourse on Development of EEG Diagnostics and Biofeedback for Attention-Deficit/Hyperactivity Disorders," *Biofeedback and Self-Regulation,* vol. 16, no. 3 (1991).

12. R.B. Smith, "Cranial Electrotherapy Stimulation," in J.B. Myklebust, J.F. Cusik, A. Samies, S.J. Larson, et al., *Neural Stimulation,* vol. 2 (Boca Raton, Florida: CRC Press, Inc., 1983), 129-150.

13. Kristin Swartz and Eric Braverman, M.D., "Cranial Electrotherapy Stimulation (CES)," *Townsend Letter for Doctors* (December 1991); E. Braverman, R. Smith, R. Smayda, and K. Blum, "Modification of P300 Amplitude and Other Electrophysiological Parameters of Drug Abuse by Cranial Electrical Stimulation," *Current Therapeutic Research* 48(4) (1990): 586-596.

14. R.B. Smith, "Confirming evidence of an effective treatment for brain dysfunction in alcoholic parents," *Journal of Nervous Mental Disorders* 170(5) (1982): 275-278.

15. Eric Braverman, Ray Smith, Richard Smayda, and Kenneth Blum, "Modification of P300 Amplitude and Other Electrophysiological Parameters of Drug Abuse by Cranial Electrical Stimulation," *Current Therapeutic Research,* vol. 48, no. 4 (October 1990), 586-596; E.R. Braverman, K. Blum, and R.J. Smayda, "A commentary on brain mapping in 60 substance abusers: Can the potential for drug abuse be predicted and prevented by treatment?" *Current Therapeutic Research* 48141 (1990): 569.

16. Hans R. Huessy, "Attention Deficit Disorder: What Is It?" University of Vermont College of Medicine, Department of Psychiatry (unpublished, 1992).

## Chapter 10

1. Merlene Miller and David Miller, *Reversing the Weight Gain Spiral* (New York: Ballantine Books, 1994), 309.

## Chapter 11

1. Charles Swindoll, *Standing Out, Being Real in an Unreal World* (Portland, Oregon: Mulnomah Press, 1983), 51–52.

2. Many of the ideas and concepts in this chapter were contributions from Anne Welch. Some have come from the book *Reversing the Weight Gain Spiral* by Merlene Miller and David Miller.

3. Quoted in Matthew Fox, *The Coming of the Cosmic Christ* (San Francisco: Harper & Row, 1988), 5.

## Appendix A

1. I. Maltzman, "Why alcoholism is a disease," *Journal of Psychoactive Drugs* 26 (1994): 13–31.

2. H. Fingarette, *Heavy Drinking* (Berkeley: University of California Press, 1988); M.B. Sobell and L.C. Sobell, *Behavioral Treatment of Alcohol Problems: Individualized Therapy and Controlled Drinking* (New York: Plenum, 1978); D.J. Armor, J.M. Polich, and H.B. Stambul, *Alcoholism and Treatment Report*, 1739 NIAAA (Santa Monica, California: Rand Corporation, 1976); S. Peele, "Alcoholism, politics, and bureaucracy: the consensus against controlled-drinking therapy in America, *Addictive Behaviors* 17 (1992): 49–62; G.A. Marlatt, "Substance abuse: implications of a biopsychosocial model for prevention, treatment, and relapse prevention," eds. J. Grabowski and G.R. VandenBos, *Psychopharmacology: Basic Mechanisms and Applied Interventions* (Washington, D.C.: American Psychological Association).

3. K. Blum, et al., "The Disease "Precept" or Reward Deficiency Syndrome; A Biogenic Model," *Journal Psychoactive Drugs* (in press).

4. J.R. Milam, "The Alcoholism Revolution," *Professional Counselor Magazine*, 8(2) (October 1993).

# Notes

## Appendix C

1. J.R. Morrison and M.A. Stewart, "The psychiatric status of the legal families of adopted hyperactive children," *Archives of General Psychiatry* 28 (1973): 888–891.

2. A.J. August, M.A. Steward, and C.S. Holmes, "A four-year followup of hyperactive boys with and without conduct disorder," *British Journal of Psychiatry* 143 (1983): 192–198.

3. Z. Weiner, A. Welner, M. Stewart, H. Palkes, and E. Wish, "A controlled study of siblings of hyperactive children, *Journal of Nervous Mental Disorders* 165 (1977): 110–117; D.P. Cantwell, "Psychiatric illness in families of hyperactive children," *Archives of General Psychiatry* 27 (1972): 414–417.

4. D.L. Pauls, S.E. Shaywitz, P.L. Krazer, B.A. Shaywitz, and D.J. Cohen, "Demonstration of Vertical Transmission of Attention Deficit, *Annals of Neurology* 14 (1965): 363; R. Lopez, "Hyperactivity in twins," Canada Psychological Assocation, 10 (1965): 421.

5. R. Lopez, "Hyperactivity in twins," Canada Psychological Association 10 (1965): 421.

6. R.C. McMahon, "Genetic etiology in the hyperactive child syndrome: A critical review," *American Journal of Orthopsychiatry* 50 (1980): 145–150.

## Appendix D

1. Developed by David K. Miller and Rick Thomas.

# Glossary

In relation to addiction and also to attention deficit hyperactivity disorder, there is some confusion about terminology. We do not want to contribute to disagreement and misunderstanding about either condition because of differences in the use of words to describe them. Our glossary will define some of the terminology we use, but we also want you to understand why we use the terms we do and the variety of terms used to describe the same or a similar condition.

What we call *attention deficit hyperactivity disorder* is sometimes referred to as *attention deficit disorder* and *attention deficit/hyperactivity disorder*. At times, we also use these terms to mean the same thing. There are two major identifying symptoms of this condition—attention deficit *and* hyperactivity. Some people are identified primarily because of one of these symptoms and some because of the other. Most often they come together but not always. Because of the many different ways this condition manifests itself we do not distinguish among types. When we use the term *attention deficit hyperactivity disorder* we refer to a general condition regardless of how it manifests itself in the person who has it.

Quotes from others who have written about attention deficit hyperactivity disorder include other terms that have been used in the past as a label for this condition: *minimal brain damage, minimal brain dysfunction, hyperkenesis,* or simply *hyperactivity*. They generally refer to the condition now commonly called attention deficit hyperactivity disorder.

Terminology and definitions relating to addiction are even more complex than those relating to ADHD. This is partially due to the complexity of addiction itself. There simply is no single or agreed-upon definition or way of categorizing addictions or addictionlike behaviors.

In this book, the term *addiction* refers to a condition in which a person has become dependent upon something and may be unable to function without it, a condition where one's physiology, behavior, and social interaction is affected in a chronic and sometimes life-threatening way. Other terms that are used for substance addictions are *chemical dependency, substance abuse, substance dependency, chemical addiction,* and *sub-*

*stance use disorders.* Terms used to refer to the substance a person is addicted to are *mood-altering chemical, mind-altering substance, addictive substance, addictive chemical, addictive drug,* or, simply, *drug* or *chemical.*

With a behavioral addiction, a behavior or set of behaviors, rather than a substance, is the object of compulsion. Behaviors as well as substances can alter mood. Behavioral addictions include fixation of thinking, feeling, and actions that produce certain "reward" payoffs in the form of altered brain chemistry. Other terms used for behavioral addictions are *compulsive disorders, process addictions,* and *compulsive behaviors.* Following are some definitions that may be helpful to you in understanding the concepts presented in this book.

**Abstinence.** Condition of not using a particular substance; refraining from using a drug, such as alcohol.

**Acetaldehyde.** A colorless liquid that is an intermediate substance formed in the metabolism of alcohol.

**Acetaldehyde dehydrogenase.** A natural enzyme in the body that aids in the conversion of dopamine aldehyde to dopamine acid, and of acetaldehyde to carbon dioxide and water.

**Addiction.** 1. A physiological dependence upon a substance, such as alcohol. 2. A pattern of behavior characterized by an overwhelming involvement with using a drug and securing its supply, despite adverse consequences associated with use of the drug, and with a significant tendency to relapse after quitting or withdrawal. The term is used frequently to describe drug dependence; chemical dependence; substance abuse; state of psychological or physical need, or both, for a drug, characterized by compulsive use, tolerance, and physical dependence as manifest by withdrawal sickness (withdrawal or abstinence syndrome).

**Agonist.** A substance that binds to a receptor and produces a physiological effect.

**Al-Anon.** An international self-help organization, founded in 1951, for the families and associates of alcoholics. It is based on the Twelve-Step Alcoholics Anonymous program and offers help to its members through discussion and information services.

**Alateen.** An international self-help organization for the children of alcoholics.

**Alcogene.** A specific gene that may lead to alcoholism.

**Alcohol dehydrogenase.** An enzyme that converts alcohols to acetaldehydes.

**Alcoholic.** A person suffering from alcoholism.

**Alcoholics Anonymous.** An international self-help group, founded in 1935, whose members are alcoholics who want to stop drinking. Their program emphasizes psychological and spiritual resources in overcoming alcoholism.

**Alcoholism.** A severe dependence on excessive amounts of alcohol; a chronic illness with a slow onset that can occur at any age. It is a biogenetic disease in at least 50 percent of the alcoholic population.

**Allele.** An alternate or abnormal form of a gene.

**Amino acid.** An organic chemical compound that contains both an amine group and a carboxyl group; the unit of structure of proteins. They exist in both essential (not produced in the body in sufficient amounts) and nonessential (synthesized sufficiently in the body) varieties.

**Antabuse.** Brand name for disulfiram, an antioxidant used in aversion therapy to create an aversion to alcohol. It builds up acetaldehyde, leading to severe nausea and potentially fatal side effects when alcohol is consumed.

**Antagonist.** A substance that binds to a receptor, has no effect on the receptor itself, but prevents the bonding of an agonist to that receptor.

**Axon.** A neuronal process that conducts impulses away from the cell body.

**Beta-endorphin.** An opioid peptide secreted by the cells of the hypothalamus and pituitary gland. It acts as a pain reliever and has behavioral effects and comprises the amino acid sequence 61 to 91 of the beta-lipotropin molecule.

**Blackout.** Early warning sign of alcoholism characterized by alcohol-induced amnesia or memory blank-out, but no loss of consciousness.

**Biogenetic.** Related to biological and hereditary factors.

**Brain wave.** Within the brain, a rhythmical fluctuation of electrical potential.

**Catecholamines.** Substances that contain the catechol function. Both dopamine and norepinephrine are catecholamines.

**Chemical messenger.** A neurotransmitter substance involved in neuronal communication.

**Chromosomes.** Structures in the nucleus of cells containing linear threads of DNA that transmit genetic information.

**Cocagene.** A specific gene that may lead to cocaine addiction.

**Compulsive.** Pertaining to a strong, often irresistible impulse to perform an act against one's will.

**Craving.** A strong desire for something, including alcohol, drugs, food, or behavioral activities.

**Disease concept.** The theory that alcoholism is a chronic illness, the onset of which is influenced by biochemical sensitivities and psychological and social factors.

**DNA.** Deoxyribonucleic acid, the substance in the chromosomes that carries the genetic code for the production of genes.

**Dopamine.** A neurotransmitter in the central nervous system and an intermediate in the synthesis of norepinephrine. It is made from amino acids and sends messages that increase well-being, aggression, alertness, and sexual excitement.

**Dopaminergic.** Pertaining to the dopamine system.

**Double-blind study.** Clinical methodology in which neither the patient nor the experimental administrator is aware of the contents of the administered substances being tested.

**D-phenylalanine.** An alternate form of an essential amino acid; inhibits enkephalinase.

**Drug.** Any substance that, upon entering a body, can change either the function or structure of the organism.

**Drug abuse.** Deliberate use of chemical substances for reasons other than their intended medical purposes and that results in physical, mental, emotional, or social impairment of the user.

**Drug dependence.** State of psychological or physical need, or both, for a drug; usually characterized by compulsive use, tolerance, and physical dependence manifest by withdrawal sickness; chemical dependence; condition often equated with addiction.

**Drug misuse.** Unintentional or inappropriate use of prescribed or nonprescribed medicine, resulting in impaired physical, mental, emotional, or social well-being of the user.

**Dynorphin.** A class of neuropeptides that are made from prodynorphin peptides. They are opioid peptides that regulate the immune response, raise the pain threshold, stimulate feelings of well-being, regulate sexual and mental activity, and reduce compulsive behavior.

**Dysphoria.** A feeling of discomfort or unpleasantness.

**Endorphin.** Any of a group of endogenous neuropeptide brain substances that bind to opiate receptors in various areas of the brain. They are involved in craving behavior, pain, sexual function, and other brain and systemic functions.

**Enkephalin.** Either of two naturally occurring pentapeptides (methionine or leucine) in the brain, that have potent opiatelike effects and serve as neurotransmitters.

**Enkephalinase.** Carboxypeptidase A, an enzyme that destroys enkephalins.

**Gene.** The unit of heredity responsible for transmission of a characteristic to the offspring. It occupies a specific place on the chromosome.

**Genetic.** Pertaining to heredity, rather than being environmentally caused.

**Genetic predisposition.** An inheritable characteristic; for example, the risk of acquiring a disease such as alcoholism.

**Glucogene.** A specific gene which may lead to carbohydrate bingeing.

**Hormone.** The chemical produced by an endocrine gland that affects the functions of specifically receptive organs or tissues when transported to them by the bodily fluids. Examples include insulin and endorphins.

**Inhibitory.** Tending to stop or slow a process. A substance that suppresses a nerve impulse is inhibitory.

**Intoxication.** Temporary state of mental chaos and behavioral dysfunction resulting from the presence of a neurotoxin, such as ethyl alcohol, in the central nervous system.

**L-dopa.** 3, 4-Dihydroxyphenylalanine, an amino acid that is the precursor to dopamine.

**Loss of control.** Inability of an alcoholic or drug user to predict consistently the length of drinking or the amount of drug consumed once use of alcohol or drugs has begun.

**Metabolize.** The chemical process that takes place in living organisms, resulting in the generation of energy, growth, the elimination of wastes, and other daily functions as they relate to the distribution of nutrients in the blood after digestion.

**Monoamines.** Amines containing one amine group derived from food and carried by the blood into the brain. Compare *neuropeptides*.

**Mutation.** A change in genetic material that is permanent and transmissible.

**Naloxone.** A narcotic antagonist; also used as an antidote to narcotic overdosage. An earlier form of Naltrexone.

**Naltrexone.** A narcotic antagonist used in the long-term detoxification of opiate addicts. It acts to block the readministration of heroin. It is an adjunct to relapse prevention.

**Narcotics Anonymous.** A self-help group patterned after Alcoholics Anonymous in which recovering drug addicts offer help to others seeking recovery from drug dependence.

**Neurochemistry.** The branch of neurology dealing with the chemistry of the nervous system.

**Neuron.** A nerve cell.

**Neuropeptides.** Neurotransmitters made from giant linked amino acids called peptides. They are inactive in this giant form but are broken down into smaller active neuropeptides in the endoplasmic reticulum.

**Neurophysiological.** Of or pertaining to the function of the nervous system.

**Opiate.** A narcotic drug that contains opium, its derivatives, or any of several semisynthetic or synthetic drugs with opiumlike activity. Opiates cause sleep, the relief of pain, and other pharmacological responses.

**Opioid peptides.** Any substance that contains more than one linked amino acid, possessing the ability to interact with one or more neural opiate receptors. These substances are usually found in the brain and act as hormones.

**Peptides.** A compound composed of two or more amino acids joined by peptide bonds.

# Glossary

**Physical dependence.** A condition in which the body requires a particular agent for normal operation, following chronic abuse of that agent, or a similar one.

**Placebo.** An inactive substance or treatment without therapeutic value, given to satisfy a patient's need for treatment. A placebo is also used in the control group of studies that test medicinal or other treatments.

**Presynaptic.** Situated or occurring proximal to a synapse. Compare *postsynaptic*.

**Psychological dependence.** Condition marked by a strong desire and intense craving to repeat the use of a drug for various emotional reasons, i.e., feeling of well-being and reduction of tension.

**P300 wave.** A specific wave form that is characteristic of an individual's response to visual stimuli. When reduced, it indicates risk of alcoholism.

**Receptor.** Molecules on the surface of cells that recognize and bond with specific molecules, producing some particular effect.

**Restriction fragment length polymorphism (RFLP).** A genetic technique that is used to detect genes responsible for genetic diseases.

**RNA.** Ribonucleic acid, a nucleic acid of high molecular weight that synthesizes proteins and acts in cell replication.

**Self-medication.** Practice of treating oneself with nonprescription medicine for relief of symptoms of a disease or disorder.

**Serotonin.** 5-Hydroxytryptophan, an important hormone and neurotransmitter found in many tissues, including the central nervous system.

**Synapse.** The junction between the processes of two neurons, or between a neuron and an effector organ, across which electrochemical messages are transmitted.

**Tetrahydroisoquinoline.** A substance formed by the metabolism of alcohol that fills and stimulates opiate receptors.

**TIQ.** Abbreviation for tetrahydroisoquinoline.

**Tolerance.** The lessening of the effect of a drug following repeated administration.

**Twelve-step program.** The principles set forth by Alcoholics Anonymous to aid members in their personal recovery.

**Withdrawal.** The process of abstaining from a certain agent to which one is addicted. Also, the symptoms caused by such abstention.

**Withdrawal symptoms.** Withdrawal sickness or abstinence syndrome consisting of drastic changes in physical functioning and behavior (insomnia, tremors, nausea, vomiting, cramps, elevation of heart rate and blood pressure, convulsions, anxiety, psychological depression) due to overactivity of the nervous system, which are observed or experienced after cessation of use of a drug by a physically dependent person.

# Suggested Readings

Amen, D. *Healing the Chaos Within.* Fairfield, California: MindWorks Press, 1995.

Blum. K., J.G. Cull, and P.J. Sheridan. "Genetic Screening: To Be or Not To Be?" *Genetic Engineering News,* vol. 15, no. 20 (1995): 4 and 31.

Blum, K., and M.C. Trachtenberg. "Addicts May Lack Some Neurotransmitters." *The U.S. Journal* (July 1987).

Blum, K., and J. Payne. *Alcohol and the Addictive Brain.* New York: The Free Press, 1991.

Cermak, L.S. "Cognitive-Processing Deficits in Chronic Alcohol Abusers." *Alcohol Health & Research World,* vol. 14, no. 2 (1990).

Comings, D.E. "The Genetics of Addictive Behaviors: The Role of Childhood Behavioral Disorders." *Addiction and Recovery* (November/December 1991): 10–13.

Comings, D. *Tourette Syndrome and Human Behavior.* Duarte, California: Hope Press, 1990.

Cook, E.H., M.A. Stein, M.D. Krasowwski, W. Cox, D.M. Olkow, J.W. Kieffer, and B. L. Leventhal. "Association of Attention-Deficit Disorder and the Dopamine Transporter Gene." *American Journal of Human Genetics* 56 (1995): 993–998.

Cowart, V.S. "The Ritalin Controversy: What's Made This Drug's Opponents Hyperactive?" *Journal of the American Medical Assocation* 259 (1988): 2521–2523.

Cowley, G., and J.C. Ramo. "The Not-Young and the Restless." *Newsweek* (July 26, 1993): 48–49.

Davis, J. *Endorphins: New Waves in Brain Chemistry.* Garden City, NY: Dial, 1984.

Erenberg, G., R.P. Cruse, and A.D. Rothmer. "Gilles de la Tourette Syndrome: Effect of Stimulant Drugs." *Neurology* 35 (1985): 1346–1348.

Fargason, R. E., and C. V. Ford. "Attention Deficit Hyperactivity Disorder in Adults: Diagnosis, Treatment, and Prognosis." *Southern Medical Journal* 87 (1994): 302–309.

## Suggested Readings

Goldstein, S., and M. Goldstein. *Managing Attention Disorders in Children: A Guide for Practitioners.* New York: John Wiley & Sons Inc., 1990.

Goldstein, S., and M. Goldstein "Attention-Deficit Hyperactivity Disorder in Adults." *Directions in Psychiatry,* vol. 15, lesson 18 (August 1995).

Gordon, M. *ADHD/Hyperactivity: A Consumer's Guide.* Dewit, NY: GSI Publications, 1991.

Gorski, T.T., and M. Miller. *Staying Sober: A Guide for Relapse Prevention.* Independence, Missouri: Herald House/ Independence Press, 1986.

Hallowell, E.M., and J.J. Ratey. *Driven to Distraction.* New York: Pantheon Books, 1994.

Hartmann, T. *Attention Deficit Disorder: A Different Perception.* Novato, California: Underwood-Miller, 1993.

Ingersoll, B.D., and S. Goldstein. *Attention Deficit Disorder and Learning Disabilities: Realities, Myths, and Controversial Treatments.* New York: Doubleday, 1993.

Langer, D.H., K.P. Sweeney, D.E. Bartenbach, P.M. Davis, and K.B. Menander. "Evidence of Lack of Abuse or Dependence Following Pemoline Treatment: Results of a Retrospective Study." *Drug and Alcohol Dependence* 17 (1986): 213-227.

Matochik, J.A., L.L. Liebenauer, A.C. King, H.V. Szymanski, R.M. Cohen, and A.J. Zametkin. "Cerebral Glucose Metabolism in Adults with Attention Deficit Hyperactivity Disorder After Chronic Stimulant Treatment." *American Journal of Psychiatry* 151 (1994): 658–664.

Mattes, J. "Propanolol for Adults with Temper Outbursts and Residual Attention Deficit Disorder." *Journal of Clinical Psychopharmacology* 6 (1986): 299–302.

Milam, J.R., and K. Ketcham. *Under the Influence.* Seattle: Madrona Publishers, Inc., 1981.

Miller, M., T.T. Gorski, and D.K. Miller. *Learning to Live Again.* Independence, Missouri: Herald House/Independence Press, 1992.

Minde, K., G. Weiss, and N. Mendelson. "A Five-Year Follow-up Study of Ninety-one Hyperactive School Children." *Journal of the American Academy of Child Psychiatry* 11 (1972): 595–610.

# Suggested Readings

Mirsky, S. "Thought Control: Can Biofeedback Improve Your Mental and Physical Performance?" *Men's Fitness* (March 1995): 104–106.

Murphy, K.R., and S. LeVert. *Out of the Fog: Treatment Options and Coping Strategies for Adult Attention Deficit Disorder*. New York: Hyperion, A Skylight Press Book, 1995.

Neher, T. "Altered (Chemical) States: A Practical Look at Brain Chemistry and Addictions." *Professional Counselor* (March/April 1991): 31–34.

Phil, R., and J. Peterson. "Attention-Deficit Hyperactivity Disorder, Childhood Conduct Disorder, and Alcoholism: Is There an Association?" *Alcohol Health and Research World* 15, no. 1 (1991): 25–30.

Ratey, J.J., M.S. Greenberg, and K. Lindem. "Combination of Treatment for Attention Deficit Hyperactivity Disorder in Adults." *Journal of Nervous Mental Disorders* 179 (1991): 699–701.

Robertson, J. "Preventing Relapse and Transfer of Addiction: A Neurochemical Approach." *EAP Digest* (September/October 1988).

Rosemond, J.K. *Ending the Homework Hassle*. Kansas City, Missouri: Andrews and McMeel, 1990.

Ryan, R.S., and J.W. Travis. *The Wellness Workbook*. Berkeley, California: Ten Speed Press, 1981.

Sasone, D., N.M. Lambert, and J. Sandoval. "The Adolescent Status of Boys Previously Identified as Hyperactive." In *Hyperactivity: Current Issues, Research, and Theory*. 2d ed. Edited by D.M. Ross and S.A. Ross. New York: John Wiley & Sons Inc., 1982.

Seamands, D.A. *Healing for Damaged Emotions*. Wheaton, Illinois: Victor Brooks, 1987.

Shekim, W.O. "Adult Attention Deficit Hyperactivity Disorder, Residual State." *Chadder Newsletter* (Spring/Summer 1990): 16–18.

Smith, D.E., and D.R. Wesson. *Treating Cocaine Dependency*. Center City, Minnesota: Hazelden, 1988.

Ullmann, R.K., and E. Sleator. "Attention Deficit Disorder: Children with or without Hyperactivity; Which Behaviors Are Helped by Stimulants." *Clinical Pediatrics* 24 (1985): 261–269.

Vinson, D.C. "Therapy for Attention Deficit Hyperactivity Disorder." *Archives of Family Medicine* 3 (1994): 445–451.

Wallis, C. "Life in Overdrive." *Time* (July 18, 1994): 42–50.

Weiss, G., and L.T. Hechtman. *Hyperactive Children Grown Up.* New York: The Guilford Press, 1986.

Weiss, L. *Attention Deficit Disorder in Adults: Practical Help for Sufferers and Their Spouses.* Dallas: Taylor Publishing Company, 1992.

Weiss, R.D., H.G. Pope, and S.M. Mirin. "Treatment of Chronic Cocaine Abuse and Attention Deficit Disorder, Residual Type, with Magnesium Pemoline." *Drug Alcohol Dependence* 15 (1985): 69–72.

Wender, P. *The Hyperactive Child, Adolescent, and Adult: Attention Deficit Disorder through the Lifespan.* New York: Oxford University Press, 1987.

Wilens, T.E., J.B. Prince, J. Biederman, T.J. Spenser, and R.J. Frances. "Attention Deficit Hyperactivity Disorder and Comorbid Substance Use Disorders in Adults." *Psychiatric Services,* vol. 46, no. 8 (1995): 761–765.

Zametkin, A.J., T.E. Nordahl, M. Gross, et al. "Cerebral Glucose Metabolism in Adults with Hyperactivity of Childhood Onset." *New England Journal of Medicine* 323 (1990): 1361–1366.

# Resources

The following are programs, organizations, or people from whom you may get more information about ADHD and/or addiction.

Attention Deficit Disorder Association (ADDA)
P.O. Box 972
Mentor, OH 44061
(800) 487-2282

Kenneth Blum, Ph.D., President
KANTROLL, Inc.
1211 Lost Stone
San Antonio, TX 78258
(210) 499-0537 or FAX (210) 490-8634

Carol Cummings, M.A., C.A.D.C. III, R.M.F.T.
Counseling and Mediation Center, Addiction Services
334 N. Topeka
Wichita, KS 67202
(316) 269-2322

C.H.A.D.D. National State Networking Committee
499 NW 70th Avenue, Suite 308
Plantation, FL 33317
(305) 587-3700

*Challenge* Newsletter
P.O. Box 448
West Newbury, MA 01985

Graceland College Addiction Studies Program
1-800-585-6310

Learning Disabilities Association of America
4156 Library Road
Pittsburgh, PA 15234
(412) 341-1515

Gary Lee
Substance Abuse Recovery Programs
330 S.W. Oakley
Topeka, KS 66605
(913) 234-3448

**Resources**

National Network of Learning Disabled Adults
(602) 941-5112

Neurofeedback Training Centers
  Newport Beach, CA
  Fullerton, CA
  Corona, CA
  Riverside, CA
Administrative Office (909) 784-4357

Kathy Sloan
Total Wellness Center, L.C.
14161 S. Mur-Len
Olathe, KS 66062
(913) 764-8409

Rick Thomas, Ph.D.
Osawatomie State Hospital
Osawatomie, KS 66064
(913) 755-3151
Home: (816) 322-4526

The 12,000 Kids Countdown Coalition
P.O. Box 50062
Irvine, CA 92619
(714) 543-2874

Dale Walters, Ph.D.
Dale Walters Biofeedback Seminars and Consulting
Topeka, KS 66621
(913) 272-4678

For information on setting up "Overload" workshops, retreats,
or camps please write to:
Miller Associates
 ox 258
  ependence, MO 64051
   (816) 254-8808